GOOD MORNING, MR CRUSOE

The Life and Strange Surprizing Adventures of
Robinson Crusoe, published in the year MDCCXIX,
which for 300 Years has instructed the Men
of an Island off the Coast of mainland Europe
to Contemn all Foreigners and Women.
Printed for CB editions in MMXIX.

Jack Robinson

First published in 2019
by CB editions
146 Percy Road London W12 9QL
www.cbeditions.com

Cover: from an 18th-century chapbook edition of *Robinson Crusoe*;
page 9: Mary Evans Picture Library/Alamy;
page 102: Huntington Library; page 149: via Public Domain Review

Jack Robinson has asserted his right
under the Copyright, Designs and Patents Act 1988
to be identified as author of this work

Printed in England by ImprintDigital, Exeter

978–1–909585–29–4

Good Morning, Mr Crusoe

Also by Jack Robinson
(a pen-name of Charles Boyle, editor of CB editions)

Days and Nights in W12
'Ingeniously observed, clever, elliptical and funny. It's like the best
moments from a novel – minus the padding.' – Geoff Dyer

by the same author
'A kind of portrait of the contemporary committed reader:
oh, you think, reading it, is *that* what I'm like?' – Jonathan Gibbs

Robinson
'Few works of literature are as delicate, poignant, erudite, playful and
profound as Jack Robinson's *Robinson*.' – Neil Griffiths

An Overcoat: Scenes from the Afterlife of H.B.
'I can't think of a wittier, more engaging, stylistically audacious, attentive
and generous writer working in the English language right now.'
– Nicholas Lezard, *Guardian*

'The most innovative, intelligent, vertiginous novel to appear
in years.' – Frances Wilson, *TLS*

Blush
with Natalia Zagórska-Thomas
'a subtle and insightful phenomenology and social history of blushing
alongside witty and equally subtle and insightful images'
– Thomas Koed, *Volume*

THE
LIFE
AND
STRANGE SURPRIZING
ADVENTURES
OF
ROBINSON CRUSOE,
Of *YORK*, Mariner:

Who lived Eight and Twenty Years,
all alone in an un-inhabited Ifland on the
Coaft of AMERICA, near the Mouth of
the Great River of OROONOQUE;

Having been caft on Shore by Shipwreck, where-
in all the Men perifhed but himfelf.

WITH

An Account how he was at laft as ftrangely deli-
ver'd by PYRATES.

Written by Himfelf.

LONDON:
Printed for W. TAYLOR at the *Ship* in *Pater-Nofter-
Row.* MDCCXIX.

Title page of the first edition of *Robinson Crusoe*, 1719

I dreamed that, laden with the honoraria of duty, in a mild clank of medals, I pottered in my shed, concealed by foliage from my cardboard house, steadily repeated along the avenue.

– Iain Crichton Smith, *The Notebooks of Robinson Crusoe*, 1975

Bury the dead. Say Robinson Crusoe was true to life. Well then Friday buried him. Every Friday buries a Thursday if you come to look at it.

– James Joyce, *Ulysses*, 1922

I am always suspicious of those decrees of providence which run parallel to the interests of persons who have taken it upon themselves to expound providential wisdom.

– Cicely Hamilton, *Marriage as a Trade*, 1909

Author's Note

Good Morning, Mr Crusoe is issued to coincide with the 300th anniversary of the first publication of *Robinson Crusoe* by Daniel Defoe in 1719. Some material from *Robinson* (CBe, 2017) is revisited. The form of the present book – an essay of sorts, followed by notes and asides, diversions and interruptions – is borrowed from Walter de la Mare's *Desert Islands and Robinson Crusoe* (1930).[1]

Thank you to Tanya Harrod and Tony Lurcock for leads to Robinsons who were not on my map, and to Lesley Levene. Thank you to Natalia Zagórska-Thomas for talking to me about the matter of Crusoe from outside my box; there are lines in here that are hers.

According to the introduction by Frederick Brereton[2] to my 1953 Collins Classics edition of Defoe's novel, 'Robinson Crusoe is a perfectly normal Englishman reacting to his unusual environment in a perfectly normal manner.' If you scratch a 'normal' white Englishman and find traces of racism, misogyny and a childish sense of entitlement – oh, good morning, Mr Crusoe.

Contents

Uxbridge Road

A cupcake with vivid pink icing and three small candles has arrived on the wobbly table on the pavement. Robinson looks confused. Using Robinson's lighter, the waitress lights the candles, then Robinson lights another cigarette. The weather this afternoon in April is damp and cold and the pain in his hips is playing up.

'Happy anniversary!' says the waitress.

She's new. She is from one of the countries that used to be coloured pink on the maps and now are not, or her parents were or her grandparents, and she is being paid the minimum wage and is studying for a postgrad degree and she is wearing laced black boots, which Robinson is staring at.

'Did you walk here?' he asks.

'I did walk,' she says. 'All the way from Ealing. The buses are on strike today, if you hadn't noticed, and the Tube. Aren't you going to blow the candles out?'

Robinson nods in approval. A public transport strike shouldn't be an excuse for people to stay in bed, he tells her, and she looks at him warily. When people tell her that hardship is character-building she wonders how much hardship, and what kind of character. People who say that suffering is good for you usually mean the suffering of others.

'Do you think I wouldn't rather be in bed?' she says. 'Or getting some proper work done? I've got two essays to finish by the end of the week. But if I hadn't come in I'd have lost my job.'

Robinson is often confused these days: by LGBT and #MeToo and ebooks and cyberspace – naturally: he didn't expect not to grow old – and by how many people are wearing ripped jeans, as if they'd just tripped and fallen while chasing a goat, but equally by the coexistence of this, all *this*, with the same default structures of power he has known through to his bones since the 18th century, his bones that now ache, his painful joints. Rheumatoid arthritis. He fumbles in his pockets for the pills he should be taking, the blue ones or maybe the yellow ones. Right now, he can't decide whether the cupcake with its child-sized candles is a joke or a mark of respect, and he doesn't know how to find out. Robinson is not a man who asks many questions.

One of the candles has gone out.

'So did you vote for Brexit or to stay in the EU?'

Robinson is not going to answer that. 'What's the point of a secret ballot if you then go telling everyone what you voted?' I think he did vote. He's not going miss out on marking an X with a stubby pencil in a rickety little plywood cubicle, the kind of thing he might have knocked up on his island with bits of driftwood. A sudden gust of wind and all those cubicles would topple over. And I'm pretty sure that he voted for Brexit.

Another of the candles flickers, gutters, and as Robinson shields it with his hands a notebook he's been writing in falls to the ground.

'Doing your accounts?' says the waitress, picking it up. 'Counting your blessings?' The pages where the notebook has fallen open are filled with little lists.

Robinson is not used to being *asked* questions. He is rarely asked, for example, Where do you come from? Why are you here? How long do you plan to stay? What was your grand-father's grandmother's maiden name? What do you want? What do you *really* want? Looking at Robinson, people take a lot for granted.

The waitress has gone over to talk to some Syrian men at another table, and Robinson's gaze has moved up from her boots to her thighs.

The traffic is lousy, congestion even worse than usual because of the strike. Every driver in their bubble: listening to music, texting, nose-picking. It's nearly 4 o'clock, school's out – the changing of the guard on the Uxbridge Road – and there's jostling and swearing and 'oh-my-god's being screamed outside the KFC and at the bus stop where, today, though the kids haven't clocked this, no buses will be stopping. A woman walks by with a hedgehog wrapped in a blanket. Kafka is in the post office, filling in forms in triplicate. Céline is in the back room of the halal butcher's, bandaging a hand that's lost two fingers to a meat saw. Muriel Spark is waving very ele-gantly for a taxi. Five minutes to deadline, Defoe is filing copy from his laptop in the Algerian café next door that Robinson doesn't go to, even though the coffee there is better, because he is a creature of habit. To the west, there's a pink in the sky over Acton that reminds him of something but he can't remember what.

'We all live on islands,' Robinson tells the waitress, and she folds her arms and looks at him: after 300 years, that's all he has to say?

We don't really know how to do this. On this shop-soiled island with its Tesco-coloured flag and its gentlemen's clubs staffed by Romanian servants and its Happy Hour clearance sales, it's all a bit makeshift. Robinson is scratching the lobe of his right ear and looking down at the pavement. He'd like to see a rat: if the rats are still here, maybe the ship isn't sinking.

He has his bags packed – nothing much in them, they rattle around – but nowhere to go. Now a second candle really has gone out and they'll have to be lit again and someone is going to tell him to make a wish before he blows them out.

Robinson tries again. 'We all live on islands, we are all marooned.'

'Some of us in more comfort than others,' the waitress replies.

'Work hard and you can achieve anything you want.'

She laughs. 'So did you want to end up here? Or did you just not work hard enough?'

1

Le Vrai Arbre

The Life and Strange Surprizing Adventures of Robinson Crusoe by Daniel Defoe was born into the world on 25 April 1719. (The feast day of St George, an early Christian martyr born in Cappadocia who somehow got to be patron saint of England, is 23 April; Shakespeare's date of baptism and my mother's birthday were both 26 April: there's a little cluster here.) Defoe wrote seven other works in 1719, as well as contributing to several newspapers, and by the end of the summer had published a sequel, *The Farther Adventures.* In 1720 he added *Serious Reflections During the Life and Surprising Adventures of Robinson Crusoe.* He was sixty years old. He needed to provide a dowry for one of his daughters, Hannah (who never, as it turned out, married). He needed cash; he needed to make ends meet.

Also in 1719, Defoe sold his shares in the South Sea Company – a company founded in 1711 to manage the national debt and awarded a contract to supply the Spanish colonies in South America with several thousand African slaves per year. Bribery, corruption and insider dealing combined with public credulity to drive the share price unsustainably high; in 1720 the South Sea Bubble burst, causing financial ruin to many investors. Defoe was in favour of the establishment of colonies for commercial reasons and, a man of his time, believed that slavery was necessary for business, but he disapproved of get-rich-quick schemes. In February 1719 – two months before the publication of *Crusoe* – he proposed in the *Weekly Journal* that instead of devoting itself to manipulating the financial market the South Sea Company should oversee the founding of a colony at the mouth of the River Orinoco on the north coast of South America: it would cost '500000 £ Sterling' and the government would be required 'to furnish six Men of War, and 4000 regular Troops, with some Engineers and 100 pieces of Cannon, and military Stores in Proportion for the maintaining and supporting the Design', but 'the Revenue it shall bring to the Kingdom will be a full amends'. A further colony, 'above 400 Leagues from the first Settlement', would 'bring home' as much gold as the Portuguese were getting out of Brazil, 'as well as to cause a prodigious Consumption of our British Manufactures'.[3] Defoe chose to locate the fictional island on which Robinson Crusoe is stranded around 40 miles from the mouth of the Orinoco and furnish it with a kindlier climate than that of the actual island on which Alexander Selkirk, the presumed model for Crusoe, was marooned; his book (no one was calling it a 'novel' at the time[4]) was a prospectus for potential investors, with glossy photos of beaches and palm trees.

Colonies were absorbing a lot of attention. In 1717 the Transportation Act provided for the transportation of criminals to the British American colonies; by 1776, when the colonies declared independence, 50,000 men, women and children convicted for crimes as minor as petty theft had been despatched to Virginia and Maryland.[5] In a sermon delivered in February 1719 in the church of St Mary le Bow, London, to the Society for the Propagation of the Gospel in Foreign Parts, Samuel Bradford, Bishop of Carlisle, denounced 'the deplorable state of the heathen world' and urged his congregation to continue their work of 'converting the Gentiles to God, and bringing them to repentance and obedience'. Taken as read, here, was that the Christian god trumps all other gods; the subtext was the perceived need to counteract the Roman Catholic influence in Spanish and French overseas territories with Protestant, Church of England missions.

As well as a prospectus, *Robinson Crusoe* was a how-to book for colonists, foregrounding practical skills and good husbandry and honest accounting, and shares in Defoe's book would have been a better investment than in the South Sea Company. The book was reprinted in May, June and August; within months of the first publication there were pirated versions on the market, and by the 19th century *Robinson Crusoe* had cruised far beyond the point where a book's success can be reckoned by the usual markers. Many of the new editions were published specifically for children. An 1868 edition was written entirely in words of one syllable, like an Oulipian exercise. From the foreword to an edition of *Crusoe* first published in 1905 (and reissued in 2006): '[Defoe's] story was not designed for children, and therefore it contained a great deal of hard reading. There was much in it, however, that was interesting to young people, and from that day to this, the marvelous tale of Robinson Crusoe has been a favorite with boys as well as men. I have rewritten the story in words easy for every child, and have shortened it by leaving out all the dull parts.'[6] As a result of the proliferating editions – which the flaws of the original attracted[7] – Defoe's book, Virginia Woolf wrote, 'resembles one of the anonymous productions of the race rather than the effort of a single mind', and during the period in which I grew up and learned to read most households in the UK in which there were books included among them a version of *Robinson Crusoe*.

The covers of the multiplying editions of *Crusoe* usually depicted a weather-beaten figure with musket and umbrella in the act of discovering the footprint in the sand that tells him he is not alone: the breaching of solitude, occasion for vast dismay.

Many of the illustrations were overtly racist: a black man bows down in the sand before Crusoe, whose hand is extended in a gesture that suggests not so much mercy as 'Rise, and do some useful work for me.'

Writing in a *Guardian* series on 'The 100 Best Novels Written in English' in 2013, Robert McCrum noted that 'By the end of the nineteenth century, no book in English literary history had enjoyed more editions, spin-offs and translations than *Robinson Crusoe*, with more than 700 alternative versions.' The making of lists is a very Crusoe activity; just one fifth of the books on McCrum's list are by women; a third are by American writers; from the literatures of countries which are not majority English-speaking but where English has been an official language since colonial times and novels are written in it, zero entries. McCrum maintains that Defoe's 'classic novel is English literature at its finest'. For myself, reading *Robinson Crusoe* is a dull plod. This book will argue that the reasons for its inclusion on any list of 'best' novels have little to do with literary merit and more because it surfed a wave of approval in which some ugly flotsam was swept up, and still is.

One of the best known of the 19th-century spin-offs was *Der Schweizerische Robinson* by Johann David Wyss, published in 1812 and translated (many times) into English under the title *The Swiss Family Robinson*. I haven't read it. Walter de la Mare tells me that 'It is full of that complacent and pacifying kind of instruction which glides into and out of the mind like water off a duck's back . . . It can be read on and on with an eye bordering on vacancy; and can be shut up without remorse.' Mr Robinson is 'infinite in resource and in sententiousness. His wilds are merely a daylong pulpit.' He and his family, 'tented in by a Robinsonian heaven, enjoy a prolonged picnic'.

Picnics I like, as long as they come without sermons, and

11. ROBINSON — Le Vrai Arbre

P. Javelle, phot., Robinson

many other people do too so there's money in this. *Le Vrai Arbre de Robinson* (above), established in a south-western suburb of Paris in 1848 and named for the Swiss Family, was one of a number of *ginguettes* – tea gardens, suburban hostelries, offering food and drink *en plein air*: see Renoir and Manet – that were popular in the mid-19th century. There were donkey rides, scenic railways, slides, live music, dancing. *Le Vrai Arbre* was a place to take your girl; and later, on Sunday afternoons, your whole family, but in Robinson's case that's not going to happen.

Zoom in on the upper tree house in the photograph and you can see a man shouting down: Robinson, in one of his guises, and there's surely someone else up there with him, because he does not exist without a narrator. He is shouting for more brandy or another bottle of champagne, but no one is listening: there's a photo being taken, and photography in this period, early last century, required effort and patience.

Foreground, left to right . . . A man in a uniform blowing a whistle, which is what people in uniform do, with his feet buried in – not snow, because there's none on the tree-house roofs, which appear to be thatched, so just a little dip in the ground. A woman wearing – *balancing* – a very flat hat. Behind her, a man who at least has something useful to *do*, which is hauling on the rope that's slung over a pulley and that takes the basket with the brandy up to the tree house. Do the customers leave a tip, a *pourboire*, in the basket before sending it down? Does Robinson? On the right, a smartly dressed man who may well be the owner or the manager of this fashionable establishment; he's not looking too fondly upon the photographer, and I imagine that what his right hand is doing in his pocket is gripping the handle of a gun, which he's about to draw. Far right, a woman who looks anxious and who reminds me of my mother. She doesn't want any gunplay here, no blood, though she'd be good at mopping it up, she's had years of that, mopping up after men, making good.

There was the Queen on TV on a wet summer Sunday, celebrating one of her Jubilees, and she looked like my mother in the 1950s waiting for a bus in the rain.

Have I any idea of what it took, to be her?

Le Vrai Arbre is, as well as a lookout post offering a perspective on a range of interconnected books, a family tree.[8] It may not be altogether *vrai*, this arboreal watering-hole in a suburb of Paris named after a fictional Swiss family that was itself named after a fictional mariner marooned on a desert island, but all family histories are made up of legends as well as facts.

At the top of the tree is Robinson Crusoe, 'born in the year 1632, in the city of York, of a good family, tho' not of that country', a castaway for twenty-eight years, a national male role model for three centuries and now widely perceived as representative of a certain stage of Western capitalism. (This is what readers do to fictional characters, place them in nonfiction narratives, which may themselves be forms of fiction in disguise; it can't be helped.) When Crusoe acquires a companion, a captive who escapes from cannibals and whose life he saves, he first assigns names – 'Friday', 'Master' – and follows up with instructing Friday in his duties and converting him to Christianity.[9] Shipwrecked, washed up on a desert island, given up for dead by all who knew him, Crusoe still manages to believe that he's master not just of his own fate but that of others too. James Joyce, who admired Defoe,[10] had Crusoe in his sights: 'The true symbol of the British conquest is Robinson Crusoe, who, cast away on a desert island, in his pocket a knife and a pipe, becomes an architect, a carpenter, a knife grinder, an astronomer, a baker, a shipwright, a potter, a saddler, a farmer, a tailor, an umbrella-maker, and a clergyman. He is the true prototype of the British colonist, as Friday (the trusty savage who arrives on an unlucky day) is the symbol of

Q in
footnote

the subject races. The whole Anglo-Saxon spirit is in Crusoe: the manly independence; the unconscious cruelty; the persistence; the slow yet efficient intelligence; the sexual apathy; the practical, well-balanced religiousness; the calculating taciturnity.'

A profit-seeking entrepreneur (as was Defoe), Crusoe diversified into pantomime, board games, film, TV, online gaming . . . On the printed page the variations upon Defoe's basic premise of man plus island continued to unfold into the following century and beyond: Christopher Palmer's *Castaway Tales* (2016) surveys Crusoe's reincarnation in fiction by, among many others, H. G. Wells, Jules Verne, Jean Giraudoux, Adolfo Bioy Casares, William Golding, J. G. Ballard, Michel Tournier and J. M. Coetzee.[11] In the process of this continual reinvention, Defoe's original template is tweaked, played with and turned upside down − roles are reversed, women take centre stage, the island itself changes shape and character − as it is used to reflect changing attitudes to race, gender, imperialism, rationality, the body and the environment. On her benign island with perfect mangoes, Giraudoux's Suzanne is scornful of Defoe's Crusoe: why did the silly man spend three months making a *table*? He wasn't hosting a dinner party. Why not just eat on the ground? In Sam Selvon's *Moses Ascending* (1975), Moses takes over a run-down house in Shepherd's Bush and has all his practical affairs attended to 'by my man Friday, a white immigrant from somewhere in the Midlands . . . He was a willing worker, eager to learn the ways of the Black man.'

Crusoe owned a plantation in Brazil and was shipwrecked and cast upon his island while on an expedition to bring slaves from Africa for his own and other plantations. Following a traditional English pattern,[12] a fortune made during the period of the slave trade was then squandered by his feckless descendants. Here is Robinson in Fielding's *Amelia*: 'Why, he is a gambler, and committed for cheating at play. There is not such a pickpocket in the whole quad.' And in Conrad's *Lord Jim*: 'Know my partner? Old Robinson. Yes; *the* Robinson. Don't you know? The notorious Robinson. The man who smuggled more opium and bagged more seals in his time than any loose Johnny now alive.' In Henry James's *The Princess Casamassima*, Robinson commits to revolution but is turned by love and gets stuck between the two: 'Mr Robinson has shot himself through the heart. He must have done it while you were fetching the milk.'

These and other latter-day Robinsons – including those of Kafka, Céline, Patrick Keiller and Chris Petit – are all, in their various guises, *anti-types* of the original, second sons of second sons whose lives are largely given over to removing themselves from the sacred aura that's attached to their forefather. They have dropped the 'Crusoe' while keeping the 'Robinson' and have good reasons for doing so. It would be rude to inquire too closely into their precise line of descent, but some of the genes still carry through. Muriel Spark's narrator in *Robinson* (1958) expands upon that 'sexual apathy' noted by Joyce: 'There is easily discernible in some men a certain indifference, not to woman precisely but to the feminine element in women, which might be interpreted in a number of ways. In Robinson I had detected something more than indifference: a kind of armed neutrality.' In Chris Petit's *Robinson* (1993), Robinson is still a busy entrepreneur, making money at the rough end of the market: by a kind of natural progression, he moves from smuggling art out of Eastern Europe and selling high in the West ('I was surprised we got away with it for so long') into making porn films for cable TV channels.

★

In Kafka's *Amerika* (written 1912–14, published 1927), Karl Rossmann – an innocent abroad – hooks up with Delamarche and Robinson, also trekking out of New York in search of work. They fleece him: they persuade him to let them sell his suit and pocket most of the proceeds. Stopping on the road next to a vast hotel, they send Karl in for bread, beer and bacon.[13] The head cook takes a shine to Karl and suggests that he invite his companions into the hotel too, but he declines, knowing that 'Robinson would besmirch everything, and Delamarche inevitably molest even this woman here'. Karl gets a job as a lift-boy in the hotel, an immigrant making good, but a month later Robinson turns up, asking for money. He's wearing a natty white waistcoat with four pockets trimmed in black - 'The pockets aren't real, mind, they just look like pockets' – and he takes Karl's hand to make him feel these non-pockets. He reeks of brandy. He says he feels sick, and he vomits, repeatedly; he has to be put to bed in the lift-boys' dormitory and then he gets into a fight, and Karl is sacked.

Robinson and Delamarche lure Karl into joining the *ménage à trois* they are enjoying (or enduring) with Brunelda – 'beautiful and enormous and wide and, because of a special corset she had on, I can show you in the chest, she was so firm all over'. You can imagine Brunelda in a film by Fellini; in fact, you can *see* Brunelda in a film by Fellini.[14] Delamarche has full privileges; Robinson is essentially a slave, a Man Friday, and Karl is to be inducted as another slave.

At the end of the (unfinished) novel, Karl has regained his freedom and joined a travelling theatrical troupe (an episode which Michael Hofmann, in the introduction to his own translation, suggests that Kafka may have intended as 'a sort of afterlife'). Robinson has not escaped; for better, for worse, for richer, for poorer, he's still bound to Delamarche.

Bardamu, the narrator of Céline's *Journey to the End of the Night* (1932), first meets Robinson when he's sent on a reconnaissance mission in what for a while was known as the Great War: 'I couldn't see his face, but his voice was different from ours, sadder, which made him sound nicer. Because of that, I couldn't help trusting him a little.' They try to get themselves captured by the enemy, surely their best hope of survival, and fail. Then Robinson is in Paris, annoyed that a wealthy woman he cadges money off has just hanged herself. Next, he's in the African rainforest: after journeying for ten days upriver to a ramshackle trading post – *Heart of Darkness* territory: 'trees bristling with living noisemakers, mutilated erections, horror' – Bardamu finds that the manager he is to take over from is Robinson, who vanishes in the night. Then he's in Detroit, where Bardamu works for the Ford Motor Company and Robinson cleans office toilets: 'He walked heavily, with a certain true majesty, as if he had been doing dangerous and in a way sacred things in the city. Actually I'd noticed that all those night cleaners had that look. In fatigue and solitude men emanate the divine.'

Back in Paris, Robinson is engaged by a family who want rid of the old woman who is living with them, but his plan – which involves a rabbit hutch and fireworks – goes wrong and he partially blinds himself. He and the old woman are sent south to Toulouse, where they live off showing mummified corpses in a crypt to tourists. Bardamu visits, and is surprised: Robinson is in work, is engaged to be married, and appears to be on track for bourgeois respectability. Fat chance. Robinson kills the old woman by pushing her down a ladder and runs out on the girl who loves him. He turns up at the mental institution on the outskirts of Paris where Bardamu is working. 'Something had happened to his face, something I'd never seen before, a kind of portrait had settled on his features, with forgetfulness and silence all around it.'

Robinson's girl arrives. Bardamu suggests a grand recon-
ciliation – a foursome: himself, his own new girlfriend,
Robinson, Robinson's fiancée – and it's a disaster. They go to a
carnival and pose together in a photographer's booth: 'A mag-
nesium flash. We all flinch. We each get a picture. We're even
uglier than before. The rain comes through the canvas roof.' In
a taxi, Robinson enjoys being shouted at by his girl and then
shouts back – 'People have told you there's nothing better than
love . . . Well, I say fuck their love!' – and then the girl shoots
him: three shots, one missing. He dies. The others carry his
body to the police station. The police inspector's secretary is
chatty: 'It gave him pleasure to be talking with educated people, for a change, instead of thugs. We didn't want to hurt his
feelings, so we stuck around.' Then they go home, stopping on
the way to drink at a canal-side bar that opens just before dawn
'for the benefit of the bargemen'.

Crusoe: 'I walk'd every where peeping and peeping about
the island.' This is also the occupation of Robinson in Patrick
Keiller's three films documenting English malaise in the 1990s
and 2000s. In *London* (1994) the narrator is invited by Robinson, a former lover with whom he once lived in 'an uneasy
bickering sexual relationship', to accompany him on a series of
meandering walks undertaken as part of Robinson's investigation of 'the problem' of London. The narrator has been living
abroad, and the film begins with his arrival back in 'dirty old
Blighty: under-educated, economically backward, bizarre. A
catalogue of modern miseries, with its fake traditions, its Irish
war, its militarism and secrecy, its silly old judges, its hatred of
intellectuals, its ill health and bad food, its sexual repression,
its hypocrisy and racism, and its indolence – it's so exotic, so
home-made'.

Robinson himself is neither seen nor heard. When he used

to travel abroad, the narrator tells us, Robinson was known as
an 'enthusiastic flâneur', but he now lives quietly and alone in
Vauxhall, where 'he listens to the gateposts at the entrance to
the park' and where shopping in the supermarket is 'an experience of overwhelming poignancy', because of the labels on the
imported goods. Robinson works two days a week as a lecturer
at 'the University of Barking'. 'He isn't poor because he lacks
money, but because everything he wants is unobtainable.' He
is 'not a conservationist, but he misses the smell of cigarette ash
and urine that used to linger in the neo-Georgian phone boxes
that appear on London postcards'.

It's 1992. IRA bombs detonate on Wandsworth Common,
in the City, at Staples Corner. Under John Major, the Tories
unexpectedly win the general election: 'The middle classes in
England had continued to vote Conservative because in their
miserable hearts they still believed that it was in their interest to do so.' There's a financial crash, and Britain exits the
ERM. The Queen opens an electricity substation, the Queen
Mother unveils a statue of Bomber Harris. Meanwhile, Robinson and the narrator set out on expeditions, often with a literary destination: Horace Walpole's house at Strawberry Hill,
or the school in Stoke Newington where Edgar Allan Poe was
a pupil. (Instead of the latter, they find the house where Defoe
wrote *Robinson Crusoe*, and Robinson is 'devastated': 'shipwreck, and the vision of Protestant isolation'.) They stay in
cheap hotels, on a houseboat with Peruvian musicians, and for
one night at the Savoy.

Robinson is at times nostalgic: 'We remembered what we
used to think of as the future.' And depressed: after the Tory
election victory, 'He would drink more and less well, he would
be ill more often, he would die sooner.' And impetuous: in
Fleet Street he has to be restrained from assaulting the Lord
Mayor. And – imagining poets and artists and musicians taking

over the City as the bankers drown in their own corruption – naively optimistic. And ingenious: he has plans to reform the game of golf 'to make it more artistic'. And restless: 'Robinson began to talk as he often did of leaving the country, but as always he had no idea of where to go.' And lacking stamina: 'Robinson tires easily. He thinks there's something the matter with his liver.' But still, resilient: 'We set off with a new sense of purpose towards Brent Park in Neasden.'

The film is composed of lingering but static shots – like *buildings*, really – in which people and traffic and seagulls move about. There's a flattening effect, perhaps because of a wide-angle or telephoto lens. Many of the scenes conform to an aesthetic that's now so familiar, so embracing, we've lost any exit: look at this fag-end junction, this waste ground whose soil is so toxic that even fast-buck developers shy away, this confusion of road signage, this office block with shattered windows, this graffiti-sprayed flyover, this all-round shabbiness – London embracing its own decay. It's beautiful, and a crime scene.

A French verb for what Keiller's Robinson and the narrator are doing as they criss-cross London and then England is *robinsonner*. The word was coined by Rimbaud in his poem 'Roman' (1870): 'Le cœur fou robinsonne à travers les romans . . .' Rimbaud is referring to the mad heart of a seventeen-year-old (he was sixteen when he wrote the poem): drinking, falling in love, intoxicated by fantasy. Rimbaud haunts Keiller's *London*: 'Sometimes I see the whole city as a monument to Rimbaud.' Hearing that the Canary Wharf development has gone into administration, Robinson adopts it as a monument to Rimbaud 'in memory of his wanderings in London's docks'. A disaffected art-college lecturer living a routine, timetabled life, Robinson is fuelled by the afterlife of the energies and freedoms he no longer has.

In three separate visits in the early 1870s, Rimbaud spent around fourteen months in London. He was 'delighted and astonished' by this city that made Paris appear provincial. He wrote parts of *Une Saison en Enfer* and of the *Illuminations* in London; he enjoyed the fog, the docklands, the Reading Room at the British Museum (used in same period by Karl Marx), getting drunk and rough sex with Verlaine. Together, they placed classified advertisements in the newspapers, offering lessons in French 'par deux Gentlemen parisiens'. They were watched by the police and by spies for both the British and the French governments.

Rimbaud's biographer Graham Robb notes his 'energetic pessimism, his tendency to embark on a project only when failure was guaranteed by the initial conditions'.

At the start of Patrick Keiller's film *Robinson in Space* (1997) Robinson has lost his university job and is living in a bedsit in Reading (Rimbaud's last address in England, in 1874), teaching English in a language school. He's depressed, and the narrator is concerned about 'the extent of his commitment to the derangement of the senses'.

By unlikely good luck, Robinson has a new project: he is recruited by an advertising agency to undertake an investigation into 'the problem' of England which will involve seven journeys (loosely based on Defoe's *A Tour thro' the Whole Island of Great Britain*). Robinson and the narrator start off on foot but soon need to buy a second-hand car, a Morris 1100. Among the places they visit: power stations, Oxbridge colleges, a detention centre for asylum seekers, car factories, Cliveden, Bletchley Park, landfill sites, HMS *Victory* at Portsmouth, an 'automated plasterboard factory', shopping centres, Poundbury, Shandy Hall, Blakenhurst prison, Montacute House (where one of six Jane Austen film or TV adaptations was being made in 1995, the year that Robinson is travelling), supermarket distribution centres, a radioactive waste dump, a windfarm, Halifax ('the first place we'd had a decent cup of coffee for months') and Blackpool (Robinson's home town, which holds 'the key to his Utopia'). Robinson – earnest, conscientious, zealous for facts – has with him a copy of *Port Statistics*, an official government publication, and the narrator duly reports a baffling amount of information about imports and exports, and about which company is owned by which, which is turn in owned by whom. The information that Henri Bergson's mother came from Doncaster, or that 'the only company that makes latex sheeting suitable for fetishware is based in Derbyshire', is parallel in its outlandishness.

Robinson in Space attempts to account for why this country, by all measures one of the wealthiest in the world, appears to be so dilapidated, destitute, shorn of hope. The UK is rich; there is wealth inequality, but that alone doesn't explain why the country is so *mean*. Early in the film the narrator suggests that 'the narrative of Britain since Defoe's time is the result of a particularly English kind of capitalism'; add in globalisation and the result is an unholy mess. Minor protest is recorded: a little Greenpeace; squatters occupying a golf course on the eve of World No Golf Day; the Queen's arrival at the Samsung plant in Billingham met by 'a small demonstration by the committee to defend socialism in South Korea'.

There are hiccups along the way. Suffering from months of bad food and bad hotels, Robinson and the narrator convalesce for two weeks in West Bromwich, courtesy of Robinson Bros, a chemical manufacturing company. Opposite a factory manufacturing lubricants they wait for a bus, and wait, and wait, and by the time the bus arrives Robinson has gone off for sex with someone he's found on the net.

Robinson, the narrator notes in late October, 'is beginning

to act strangely': he is planning to steal 'a piece of equipment' from one of the British-built combat aircraft that are to be sold to Saudi Arabia. (Rimbaud was once diagnosed as suffering from 'ambulatory paranoia'; Robinson has a similar affliction.) Unemployment in Middlesbrough, Robinson states through the narrator, is 17 per cent, 'the highest in the country, which has the least regulated labour market in the industrialised world and the highest prison population in Europe'. Robinson also tells the narrator that 'the plutonium aftermath of the nuclear industry will remain lethal for a quarter of a million years. At Wordsworth's birthplace I [the narrator] thought he was going to go in and register a complaint.' A few days later, the contracts of Robinson and the narrator are terminated.

In *Robinson in Ruins* (2010),[15] the final film in Patrick Keiller's trilogy, Robinson is even less present than previously: 'When a man called Robinson was released from Edgcott open prison, he made his way to the nearest city and looked for somewhere to haunt.' Robinson has vanished. The film purports to have been assembled from the cans of film and a notebook that Robinson has left behind in a derelict caravan.

Robinson still believes that he is working to a brief, this time on behalf of 'non-human intelligences' interested in the possibilities of survival for life on Earth. The prospects are not looking good. Lingering shots of flowers, lichen, butterflies and insects – Robinson is 'inclined to biophilia' – are accompanied by species-extinction statistics. Swathes of the countryside are fenced off and given over to nuclear and weapons research centres, or depots supplying aviation fuel to US and UK military bases. Doggedly, Robinson's notebook records details of local rebellions against land enclosures from the late 16th century onwards. The first time I watched the film I dozed off on the sofa, lulled by the quietly insistent voice of a pub bore; when I woke, Robinson had discovered an abandoned cement works in the Cherwell valley which he was proposing as the site of 'an experimental settlement' for the development of 'ways to reform land ownership and democratic government'.

★

In contrast to Crusoe, who was named on the title page of the first edition of Defoe's novel as not just subject but author, the latter-day Robinsons are rarely centre stage, relating directly to their audience. We see Robinson through others: through Karl Rossmann, through Bardamu, through the narrators of Muriel Spark's and Chris Petit's novels and those of the films of Patrick Keiller and the poems of Weldon Kees. Spark's brisk, highly organised narrator is frankly disappointed: 'If you choose the sort of life which has no conventional pattern you have to try and make an art of it, or it is a mess.'

Robinson swims into and then out of focus. He rings your doorbell and runs away.

It must be hard, being part of a family with such an illustrious forebear, someone you can never measure up to so why even try. It must take it out of you. Crusoe himself amassed such gravitas – or rather, his emblematic status in British culture became so far-reaching – that the natural development of his descendants was inescapably stunted. In their separate ways, all the latter-day Robinsons are children: stomping off in a huff when they don't get their own way; playing with guns, obsessed with statistics, unable to sustain any relationship based on mutual love and affection. *Family* is not a word that rhymes with either Robinson or Crusoe.

A latter-day Robinson is bound to rebel against grandfather Crusoe, but it was Crusoe who himself set this pattern: he deliberately went against the wishes of his father, who forbade him to go to sea. Crusoe's father, who 'got a good estate

use: the father's disrepair

by merchandise', comes across as a well-balanced sort of chap, bourgeois and happy to be so, urging 'the middle state' of life as 'the most suited to human happiness, not exposed to the miseries and hardships, the labour and sufferings of the mechanick part of mankind, and not embarrass'd with the pride, luxury, ambition and envy of the upper part of mankind'. He took his paternal responsibilities seriously. Yet not just Crusoe but also one of his two older brothers rebelled against this father: he ran away to join the army, and was killed in a battle against the Spanish. As for the second brother – and this is not a little strange: Defoe inserts him only to immediately delete him; he was as careless about this family as was Crusoe – 'What became of my second brother I never knew any more than my father or mother did know what was become of me.' This is not exactly the family you see in the ads for retirement investment plans.

Even rebellion is a family tradition, not a way of breaking free from that. In *Jack Robinson* (1933) by George Beaton,[16] Robinson's father has died and the family house has burned down before the end of the first page. To escape from his mother – 'the state of my clothes and my general respectability and decorum were the chief pegs of her existence' – Robinson decides to run away to sea, but before the sea even comes into sight he falls in with a shifting band of tramps, beggars, pimps and prostitutes, and he remains with them until the final page of the book, when he returns home, where his mother is 'ironing some white shirts and chatting to a neighbour'. The most lively conversation in the book is between the teenage Robinson and a woman who, before she takes him to bed, tells him 'it never rains but I wish the rain would go on coming down until it covered the whole world and everyone on it was drowned or turned into fishes . . . I love destruction.'

Beaton's Robinson is distinguished by a paralysing inertia. While begging on the streets of London, he is offered work as a cabin boy on a steamer bound for South America, but 'My feet were chained to these flat grey pavements, my eyes were riveted to these smoke-plumed houses – for among them rather than within me seemed to lie the conflicts that were just now engaging me and which did not leave me sufficient energy to part from them. Unsatisfactory as I felt my life to be at this time, I had neither the desire to evade it nor the force to alter it.' Grandfather Crusoe's assumption of agency is drained entirely; this is a Robinson alienated both from society and from himself.

Jack Robinson carries the bleak suggestion that there is no sea to run away to – that the only places you get to when you run are dosshouses and begging on the streets, and the only escape from those is back to a mother who is ironing shirts and chatting over the garden fence. She takes in washing and ironing for cash, I assume, given that to the reader's knowledge there is no man in her life except her runaway son.

Families are complicated. (*People* are complicated.) Cousins emigrate; certain uncles are never spoken about; fathers are not always, strictly speaking, fathers. Several times my mother attempted to nail down our own family tree, tracing the previous generations who migrated from Ireland (supposedly) to the west of Scotland and then across to the east and then down to the north of England, and each attempt petered out. The names – so many Johns, so many Marys – merged or dispersed or vanished; it's why simple, stark figures in made-up landscapes stand out and are looked to. My mother kept many lists, as did Crusoe:[17] of 'the comforts I enjoy'd, against the miseries I suffer'd' ('like debtor and creditor'); of the wet times of year and the dry ones; of the number of cannibals killed (this last list 'more precise by far than most butcher's bills,' notes Walter de la Mare). When Virginia Woolf noted that

Crusoe 'is for ever counting his barrels, and making sensib
provisions for his water supply', she was not mocking, and nor
am I. My mother also kept used paper bags, neatly folded, pat-
ted down flat in a drawer. What are drawers for? Receipts and
recipes, scissored neatly from newspapers; certificates, spoons,
buttons, paper clips and tape measures and rock-hard tubes of
superglue and stopped watches. Sheets: when they got worn,
she cut them in half and sewed sides to middle. Clothes: hand-
me-downs, obviously. Petrol: at the top of Harewood Hill my
mother would switch off the engine and we'd coast down,
gloriously, costing nothing. I look at the recycling bins at the
end of my street today and I know she would have approved.
She kept rows of tinned food in a kitchen cupboard – beans,
tomatoes, pilchards – with price stickers in shillings and pence,
years after decimalisation. They were being saved for when
things run out, for when the dotted line comes to an end but
with a little foresight can be prolonged, another dot and then
another. For the edge, to push it out a bit; for a rainy day. Long
before anyone had uttered the phrase 'climate change', the
prospect of *rainy days* loomed large in my mother's world view.
Marooned in her widowhood, my mother herself was Crusoe:
making do with what resources were to hand, building her
stockade, constructing a purposeful life.

Defoe's novel – which has sold a lot of copies but so have
the novels of Jeffrey Archer and Dan Brown – works as a simple tale of survival in desperate circumstances, and for that it
will continue to appeal.[18] But though Crusoe saved himself, he
couldn't save others and nor should he have ever been expected
to. As a role model for how to live with others, in society,
he was the wrong man – and not just a poor selection but *so*
the wrong man. He came with racist, imperialist and misog-
ynist baggage, and while those aspects have been edited out
of the photoshopped version – except when they have been

celebrated – they have always been there: Crusoe doesn't stand up without them. The consequences of elevating Robinson into a national role model have been, for what Frederick Brereton understood as a 'normal' Englishman, damaging; for women and non-white people even more so.

In the street, on buses and the Tube, I catch sight of Crusoe's descendants most days: white men of a certain age, a little awkward in their gait. There's a local Robinson who sometimes knocks on my door on Friday, calls me Raymond and asks to borrow a tenner, 'just to get me through the weekend, you'll get it back on Monday, promise'. And here is one of my mother's Robinsons. Early in her long widowhood, some of her well-meaning friends would invite her to dinner parties and try to set her up with an eligible widower. The wife of this particular Robinson had died from the complications of alcoholism, and people felt sorry for him. He drove an ancient Bentley and was said to own a yacht, or maybe a plane. There were walks in the Yorkshire Dales, where he had a house. He took us all for a meal at a local hotel and then, coming home, attempting a right turn off a busy main road, stalled the Bentley between the opposing streams of fast-moving traffic: I thought we were going to die. My mother finally decided that the person everyone should be feeling sorry for was the alcoholic wife.

2

Schooldays

I have no memory of reading *Robinson Crusoe* when I was a child – I think I just inhaled it – but for generations of children, girls as well as boys,[19] it has been a deeply influential book and has often been passed down like a family heirloom. Jonathan Franzen's father, who 'was born in a rough town built by his pioneer father and uncles, and he'd grown up working in road-building camps in the boreal swampland', read the novel aloud to his son; he saw in Crusoe a kindred spirit, as Franzen spelled out in an article in *The New Yorker*: 'Like Crusoe, my father felt isolated from other people, was resolutely moderate in his habits, believed in the superiority of Western civilization to the "savagery" of other cultures, saw the natural world as something to be subdued and exploited, and was an inveterate do-it-yourselfer. Self-disciplined survival on a desert island surrounded by cannibals was the perfect romance for him.' Mr Franzen was not untypical of many white middle-class fathers.

My own children have not read *Crusoe*, nor have I ever suggested that they do so.[20] There's not much of a story and the writing is pedestrian. Walter de la Mare, an admirer of Defoe, struggles to defend the style: 'The best perhaps that can be said of Defoe's prose is that it served his multifarious purposes; but as he seldom seems to have attempted feats much beyond his workaday scope, it is apt to sink below a certain level rather than to rise above it . . . careful and careless by turns, his style is as copious as easy talk, an occasional pedantry jutting up out of the raciest idioms.' Defoe's is the kind of bluff, fancy-free way of writing that most buyers of books are comfortable with; Crusoe's father, buying his round at the bar in the golf club, would have approved: books as *improving*, vaguely, if you have time for them; books as a form of self-help. 'So he proses on,' Virginia Woolf writes of Defoe, filtering everything through his own 'shrewd, middle-class, unimaginative eyes. There is no escaping him. Everything appears as it would appear to that naturally cautious, apprehensive, conventional, and solidly matter-of-fact intelligence . . .'

Robert Louis Stevenson compared *Crusoe* with Samuel Richardson's *Clarissa*, which he considered 'A book of far more startling import, worked out, on a great canvas, with inimitable courage and unflagging art. It contains wit, character, passion, plot, conversations full of spirit and insight, letters sparkling with unstrained humanity . . . And yet a little story of a shipwrecked sailor, with not a tenth part of the style nor a thousandth part of the wisdom, exploring none of the arcana of humanity and deprived of the perennial interest of love, goes on from edition to edition, ever young, while *Clarissa* lies upon the shelf unread.' After re-reading *Crusoe* in 1926, E. M. Forster noted in his *Commonplace Book*: 'an English book, and only the English could have accepted it as adult literature: comforted by the feeling that the life of adventure could be led by a man duller than themselves. No gaiety wit or invention. (Contrast Friday with Amy in Roxana; or the two storms). Boy scout manual . . . As much bored as I was 30 years ago.'

But *Crusoe* was not elevated to the canon for its literary style.

In *Emile* (1762), Jean-Jacques Rousseau described *Crusoe* as 'the most felicitous treatise on natural education' ever written. From the age of around thirteen – puberty, when clues from anywhere about gender and sex might be helpful, not to say necessary – Emile is instructed to read *Robinson Crusoe* and, for a long time, no other book: 'I want it to make him dizzy . . . I want him to think he is Robinson himself, dressed in his skins, wearing a large cap, carrying a large saber and all the rest of the character's grotesque equipment, with the exception of the parasol, which he will not need.' But the text that will provide 'both Emile's instruction and entertainment' is to be 'disencumbered of all its rigmarole' – Rousseau prescribes the central section only, 'beginning with Robinson's shipwreck near his island and ending with the arrival of the ship that comes to take him from it'. The slave-trading is cut out; and this treatise on 'natural education' will be presented without any acknowledgement that women even exist.[21]

For Rousseau, Crusoe's isolation was the whole point: 'The surest means of raising oneself above prejudices and ordering one's judgements about the true nature of things is to put oneself in the place of an isolated man and to judge everything as this man himself ought to judge of it with respect to his own utility.' I'd argue with that (and I wonder about 'utility'; but it's a bit late now): I think prejudices *harden* in isolation, and that encountering people who arrive in your own life from very elsewhere, all with their own odd convictions and blind spots, is a surer way of freeing oneself of them. As a way of teaching someone how to live well with others, in society, isolation – not least from the opposite gender – is perverse.

More generally, the island narrative of *Crusoe* was deemed by those who decided these things to be an ideal educational text, teaching the virtues of self-reliance, careful management of resources and trust in the overall – if always a little mysterious,

but that's a part of the appeal – wonderfulness of the Christian god. (Why doesn't God, all-powerful, simply kill off his
enemies, including the Devil? asks Friday, a good question.
Crusoe is briefly stumped, but does arrive at the *right answer*:
everyone has to be given the chance to recognise how wicked
they are, and repent.) In 1899 the American Unitarian minister Edward Everett Hale[22] declared: 'I regard a knowledge
of every detail of the original *Robinson Crusoe* as well-nigh
a necessity in education. Girls may occasionally be excused,
but never boys.' For Hale (in *Boys' Heroes*, 1886), Crusoe was
exemplary both for his self-reliance – 'he does so much for
himself, and has not to rest on others' – and as a model of
Christian repentance: 'He makes mistakes, he commits crimes,
he sinks in vices – and he tells of them. He repents, he turns
about, he gains strength from the Fountain of Strength – and
he tells us that, just as simply.' That the novel could also be
harnessed to the business of empire was a further recommen-
dation, as the introduction to a 1900 Cambridge University
Press edition happily declares: 'One great secret of the charm
of *Robinson Crusoe* is that in the hero of the story we recognize
those qualities of resourcefulness, activity and practical common sense that have made Great Britain the greatest colonizing power in the world. The act of "making the best of things"
was one that Englishmen had to learn when they went out to
plant the flag of England in the waste places of the earth.'

After my father died when I was aged five, my mother's
decision to send me to an all-boys boarding school at the age
of eight – a decision taken, I believe, after discussion with my
uncles but not my aunts – was a calculated (and well-meaning)
act of shipwreck. Away from home comforts, I would learn
self-reliance; boarding school also averted the risk that I might
become, as the phrase of that time had it, tied to my mother's apron strings. Standard-issue Anglican Christianity in the

background was not to be argued with. Well into my teens, I was being sent during the summer holidays on all-boys camping trips – 'expeditions' – to the Outer Hebrides.

In 1903 Thomas Godolphin Rooper – educated at Harrow and Oxford, a schools inspector for twenty-five years – celebrated the relevance of *Crusoe* to education: 'Nothing, not even football, will do more to maintain and extend the dominion of the Anglo-Saxon than the spirit of Defoe's *Robinson Crusoe*, which may be summed up in this piece of advice: "Never look to others to do for you what you can do for yourself."'

Did Rooper, I wonder, bake his own cakes, wash his own dishes, darn his own socks, make his own furniture, mend his own roof, milk his own goats? Perhaps he was blind. That summary of Crusoe-ism is a mockery of the kind of self-reliance taught to me at my own schools.

Crusoe is born 'of a good family' and raised for 'a life of ease and pleasure': 'I had never handled a tool in my life.' But on his island there are no others to look to, and here are some of the things that he makes for himself: a raft (to salvage material from the shipwreck), a tent (made from sailcloth), fences, turf walls, shelves, a chair, a table, boxes, baskets, a cage for his parrot, clothes, an umbrella, a canoe, a grindstone (operated with his feet, 'that I might have both hands at liberty'), candles, a sieve, a spade. He breeds goats and plants barley and rice. He'd like to make bread, but 'I neither knew how to grind or make meal of my corn, or indeed how to clean it and part it; nor if made into meal, how to make bread of it, and if how to make it, yet I knew not how to bake it'. By the end of his third year he has figured it all out – how to improvise sieve and mortar and pestle, how to glaze his earthenware and make an oven – and he is eating bread. Crusoe is inventive and industrious; moreover, in his work (and work, or the semblance of work, is almost entirely what he is about) he contrives to be genderless: along with hunting, he does all the things – cleaning, sewing, cooking, washing – that in the society he came from, and largely still now, were deemed women's work.

Manufacture didn't come easily to Crusoe. There was a lot of trial and error. It takes him a week to make a spade ('which when it was done was but a sorry one indeed') and two months – and the happy accident of the clay being burned in a fire – to make a couple of pots ('what odd, misshapen, ugly things'). Likewise with his clothes: 'So I set to work a-tailoring or rather, indeed, a-botching, for I made the most piteous work of it.' He decides to make a boat, and embarks on this project 'the most like a fool that ever man did, who had any of his senses awake': twenty days to fell a tree, fourteen to strip the trunk, a month to shape the underside and another three months to hack out the inside; and then, his boat being a hundred yards from the sea and too heavy to move, he realises that to cut a channel 'to bring the water up to the canoe' will take him 'ten or twelve years' – 'with great reluctancy, I gave this attempt over'. All of this is as much improvisation and play as work, as Robert Louis Stevenson noted: 'Crusoe was always at makeshifts and had, in so many words, to *play* [Stevenson's italics] at a great variety of professions.' Walter de la Mare remarks that readers love these parts of the novel 'because we have most of us tinkered up a rabbit-hutch or hung a picture' – hobbyists, all of us. Lacking the right tools for his projects, the work of realising them becomes a form of experimental performance art, as Crusoe himself recognises: it takes him forty-two days to make 'a board for a long shelf, which I wanted in my cave; whereas two sawyers, with their tools and a saw-pit, would have cut six of them out of the same tree in half a day'. Time and money are both irrelevant. At the end of the novel Crusoe is a wealthy man – but his wealth has accrued not from his own labour but from that of his slaves on his plantation in Brazil.

As with other forms of play, many of Crusoe's DIY projects appeal because they float free of economic necessity. He does need some clothes – but a 'wast-coat'? An umbrella? Something to put his knick-knacks on would be useful, but does he really need to start by spending three days cutting down a whole tree, and does the shelf really need to be 'smooth and flat as a board from end to end'? An 1874 Currier and Ives print of Crusoe sitting on an armchair in his cabin and surrounded by domesticated animals (see page 149) is an illustration in a garden-centre catalogue: shady bower, tools, equipment, a neatly edged path. There are several ironies to be unpicked here. First, many of Crusoe's labours were as much role playing as work, or work for the sake of occupying time. Second, the earnest Victorian schoolmen who considered the labours to be an exemplary form of self-reliance taught their charges to be dependent on the work of servants and women. Third, in fitting out his cabin so comfortably, and in timetabling his daily activities so religiously, Crusoe was recreating the life of security, routine and respectable appearance that he had fled England to escape from.

I've made some odd things myself, for the sheer pleasure of it: toys, ships in bottles, a kennel for my cats. But at school, where the syllabus was stripped of exactly the parts that a child might most enjoy, I never even washed my own clothes. During my entire private-school education the sum total of things I made with my hands and basic tools comprised a pair of bookends and half a rug. I enjoyed the art room for a while, until it was decided I should be doing extra Latin instead. I never learned how to cook a meal or tend a garden or make a pot, or how a TV or a car engine or a human body actually works, or how to play a musical instrument or sing or dance. I could mend a puncture in a bicycle tyre, just about. I could read Latin and some Greek, and I could march and salute. As for *making things*, that's what the working class was for. So much for self-reliance. The Crusoe I was being sold was the luxury safari version, with servants and air-conditioned Land Rovers.

Within the state school system from 1944 to the mid-1970s, children were allocated places at grammar schools, secondary modern schools or technical schools according to how they scored in the 11-plus exam. Around 30 million children took the 11-plus and under 10 million 'passed' – that is, were awarded places at grammar schools, whose academically oriented syllabus facilitated entry to university and the professions and thereby enabled some upward social mobility. There were no retakes and effectively – because of the limited number of grammar school places – no appeal. The system favoured children from middle-class homes with books on the shelves. Grammar schools: literature, Latin, complex maths and 'abstract concepts'; secondary modern: 'practical skills'; technical schools, the sciences, but in practice there weren't many of these schools (lack of money, lack of qualified teachers), so essentially just two tiers. Writing in the *Guardian* in 2017, Chris Horrie recalled the day in 1967 when he learned that he had failed the 11-plus and would be going to a secondary modern:[23] 'This was a shock. At age 11 it had been scientifically determined that I was stupid. I remain to this day a member of that segment of the British population who are not only dim-witted but officially clueless, with a letter from the government to prove it. That was just the way of it – a stone-cold, independently verified, rock-hard fact. I went upstairs to my bedroom, drew the curtains and sobbed for days.' For all its nod to Crusoe the manufacturer, able to knock up his own furniture and clothes, the education system's interest in Crusoe had nothing to do with manual labour, skilled or unskilled; it was to do with maintaining the class hierarchy and extending 'the dominion of the Anglo-Saxon'.

Generationally, what was happening at my own school was a kind of deskilling, because my father did make things. He left school aged fourteen to work in an iron foundry where his own father was a director, having married the boss's daughter; the foundry made cast-iron drainpipes and gutters and rainwater headers. He knew about crops and animals too, and about seasons and the land, because after he became a director of the foundry he bought a farm. If my father and I were marooned on separate islands, I know which one of us would survive.

Crusoe's daily routine during his third year on the island comprised, first, 'reading the Scriptures,[24] which I constantly set apart some time for thrice a day'; second, 'going abroad with my gun for food, which generally took me up three hours every morning, when it did not rain'; third, 'the ordering, curing, preserving, and cooking what I had kill'd or catch'd for my supply'. Then came planting, basket weaving, pot making: always a *next* thing to do. 'I was very seldom idle,' Crusoe boasts, and this part of Crusoe-ism was faithfully reproduced in English boarding schools. Pupils' lives were timetabled to within a half-hour, twenty minutes, of 'free' time – which is the space for music, boredom, rebellion and silliness, and the timetablers know this.

Locked into the timetabling of daily life in English boarding schools is the matter of uniform, of what clothes are permitted and when. At the public school[25] I attended between the ages of thirteen and seventeen: blue shorts, white shirts, red blazers. White shorts for certain occasions: as, for instance, being outside school grounds on weekdays, or being beaten if you'd been caught smoking cigarettes (the white shorts were thinner than the blue ones; smoking a pipe, by the way, was fine, as long as you were a prefect or in the sixth form and smoked at a certain time in a certain room). Kilt and a shirt with a studded collar and tie and a certain type of jacket for some occasions, with a different jacket for others.

The wardrobe of Defoe's Crusoe was not so elaborate: 'a great cap for my head' and 'a wast-coat and breeches open at the knees, and both loose', all fashioned from animal skins, and a folding umbrella. Michel Tournier's Crusoe in *Friday, or The Other Island* (1967) had a more sophisticated understanding of ritual: having built a 'fragile but neat' hut, he becomes conscious of 'its symbolic, and above all moral, importance', and makes a habit 'of only entering it in suitable attire, jacket, breeches, stockings and shoes, as though he were paying a formal call on what was best in himself'.

Habits and customs become traditions and rules. Tournier's Crusoe follows through: on Day 1,000 of his stay on the island he composes a Charter, incorporating a number of laws (Article 3 states that 'It is forbidden to perform one's natural functions except in the places reserved for that process'). Next, there has to be a penal code stipulating punishments for transgressions of the laws ('Whosoever pollutes the island with his excrement shall fast for one day'). Next, there probably has to be a system for revising those laws that, as circumstances change, become unworkable or plain daft. Tournier's Crusoe didn't get as far as this; after the arrival of Friday his whole system began to break down. Nor, at my own first boarding school (aged eight to thirteen),[26] do I remember feeling any need for reform: I liked the rules, the more the better, because by codifying the world into right and wrong, black and white, they told me where I was.[27] Rules made the world as tidy as a well-maintained stamp collection.

There were nights in the dormitory of that school when – silently, so as not to wake anyone else – I cried myself to sleep. I wasn't homesick. I was half an orphan: semi-marooned, on neither the ship nor the island. Whole orphans lived in the grey building at the top of the village back home;[28] non-orphans were everyone else. Not many nights: the self-pity was such a luxury, so delicious – not least because I knew that in some not-spelt-out way it was forbidden – that I rationed it. It was a form of wanking.

On the steps down to the basement room where we played table tennis I was asked by another boy if my father had died in the war – biologically not possible but there was status on offer here, a brush with heroism, and I said yes.

Off that room in the basement was another, with a TV, where we (the seniors, aged thirteen) were allowed to watch *Perry Mason* on Sunday nights. Off that room was another, bare brick walls and unfinished floor, where some of us played around with each other.

There was also a library, which (for eight-to-thirteen-year-olds) subscribed to *Punch*, *The Spectator* and the *Illustrated London News*; smuggled-in copies of *Mad* magazine were subject to confiscation. There were leather armchairs. It was a junior version, lacking waitresses bringing you a whisky-and-soda, of a gentlemen's club.

A handwritten list (a Crusoe activity) of 'Books Read in the Last Year' made in 1962 or '63, when I was aged eleven or twelve, includes around forty titles. I was cheating a bit – I don't think I hunkered under the sheets with a torch after lights-out with *Henry V* or *Julius Caesar* or *Oliver Twist*, I think we read those in class – but almost all the others I do remember reading. Here's a summary: ten titles by C. S. Forester (including books in the Hornblower series I hadn't already read); three titles each by John Buchan, Conan Doyle and Jack London; two each by H. G. Wells and Rider Haggard; one each by Kipling, Walter Scott, Victor Hugo, Alistair MacLean, Hammond Innes, Robert Louis Stevenson, Baroness Orczy, Rosemary Sutcliff, Eric Williams (*The Wooden Horse*), J. H. Williams (*Elephant Bill*), Spencer Chapman (*The Jungle Is Neutral*), Lew Wallace (*Ben Hur*), Joseph Kessel (*The Lion*), Richard Collier (*The Sands of Dunkirk*), C. M. Nelson (*He Went with Wellington*) and Anthony Richardson (*One Man and His Dog*). Also a book on Alexander the Great and another on El Cid (presumably a film tie-in). I wasn't always so literary – another year, laid up with mumps in the sickroom, I binged on fourteen Hammond Inneses – and nor was I academically bright: my school reports ran along the lines of (genuine quote) 'No flair, but he plods on', a verdict that to my mother was wholly respectable, indeed reassuring. There are just two women writers on this list, one non-English-language writer and only one book, I think, that

Mini-Crusoes: prep school, *c.*1950

was specifically written for children (Sutcliff's *The Eagle of the Ninth*). 'Young adults' hadn't yet been invented; nor, of course, had PlayStations, Xboxes, the internet and smartphones.

This is a middle-class white boy's list: war and animals, mostly.[29] (What, during this period, in the parallel universe to which I had no access, were girls reading?) A number of the books fall into the category described by Francis Spufford (in *The Child That Books Built*) as 'books theoretically for grown-ups that nonetheless showed adult men doing things that were perfectly intelligible in the context of an all-male boarding school, like escaping from Colditz'. The list includes many very good books but it reeks of conformity; it was reading-by-numbers.

One chilly, blustery afternoon during the school holidays[30] in the early 1960s my mother and I took our dog for a walk at Beamsley Beacon in Yorkshire. We were walking towards the stile in the drystone wall we had to climb over to get into the fields when we encountered another woman with another boy, and they had two large dogs which showed an aggressive interest in our own small dog. My mother shouted at the woman, telling her to keep her dogs under control. The woman shouted back. The other boy and I went to the same school. A few weeks before, he'd taken me to a quiet place – the gym, whose ropes that I had to climb gave me nightmares, and where on Wednesdays the whole school sat on hard chairs and watched Norman Wisdom comedies or patriotic war films – and asked me to show him my willy, and I did, on the back row of those hard seats, and there was nothing odd or special about this but it wasn't something you told your mother about. On that afternoon at Beamsley Beacon we didn't speak, Robinson and I, but we surely exchanged a look of despair at the mortifying behaviour of parents.

I was in my early teens. I think now that my mother shouted not because the other woman had a more flashy car and two big dogs compared to our small one – she was used to that – but because she felt herself bewildered by changes in both me and the world that were too sudden. The future was something you could put off until it happened but now, in the 1960s, it was getting mixed into the present.

My mother was born, raised, educated, employed, married and widowed within an area of ten square miles. This was a local world – an island, almost. Its boundaries were porous – the Second World War took people away, and not all of them returned – but on the whole the landmarks remained the same for succeeding generations. After my father died in 1956 my mother had to learn how to hold the financial reins, a respon- sibility she could never have expected to shoulder – money was men's territory: numbers, maths, hard facts – but which she carried out in a way that puts the investment bankers to shame. (In *Robinson Crusoe*, Crusoe's financial affairs during his prolonged absences are managed with constant diligence and honesty by a widow friend: my mother.) Her caution, her generosity too – and how these work together, and can work very well, is complicated – were derived, she said, from her Methodist upbringing, and she claimed to see both these attributes as handicaps, as if without them (but the idea of *as if* was fantasy, luxury, to be battened down) she could have had a different life.[31] The caution also had to do with wartime rationing,[32] which lasted long after the war itself ended.

The constriction of this world for a long time was not an issue because nothing happened very fast and whole lifetimes could be lived without any edge being reached, but in the 1960s my mother was under pressure. Two of my cousins became airline hostesses, glamorous at the time, and sped around the world. Sex and drugs and rock'n'roll were becoming mainstream.

In 1966, John Lennon remarked that the Beatles were more popular than Jesus; the England football team, bless them, won the World Cup; and three policemen were shot dead a few streets away from where I'm writing this now, in Shepherd's Bush (and one of the killers went into hiding for ninety-six days in Epping Forest, having learned Crusoe-like survival skills and a taste for killing during his army service in Malaya). Also that year, though not headline news: W. G. Sebald came to England to teach in Manchester, and Patrick Keiller's Robinson arrived in London, 'attracted by the period's popular culture, and the presence of so many prehistoric structures in the landscape'. Andy Warhol announced (or didn't, but because it's so characteristic the attribution has stuck) that in the future everyone would be world-famous for fifteen minutes, a promise that to my mother must have been mystifying: why would anyone *want* to be famous? And I, after coasting through the late 1950s ('he plods on'), was emerging from the feudal system of childhood into adolescence, Early Modern, where the world was not flat but confusingly and interestingly round.

Further reading. (Reading a book is like marooning oneself on an island; it doesn't make one a particularly sociable person.) At the next school – run according to the bleak ethos of its 19th-century founder, Crusoe correctness gone mad: cold showers, no heating in the dormitories, burnt porridge, corporal punishment part of the daily routine and senior boys permitted to administer this on junior boys – I began forcing the pace. I read Lowry's *Under the Volcano* before knowing what it is to be properly drunk. In March 1967, according to the date on the fly leaf, I read Faulkner's *As I Lay Dying* (and lent the book to another boy who in 2016, 49 years later, found it on his shelves, looked me up on the net, and returned it to me in a London wine bar; he still hadn't read it). My mother posted to me, wrapped in plain brown paper and with a sigh audible across 200 miles, the Updike novel I'd asked her to send, with a drawing of a naked female on the cover. Back at home, she and I sat together on the sofa watching *Play for Today* on TV (David Mercer, David Rudkin, Dennis Potter), and during one of Pinter's pauses she remarked, looking at her watch and having reckoned that in terms of words per minute she wasn't getting good value, 'He's getting *paid* for this.'

In a tiny bookshop in the Arndale Centre in Headingley I bought a copy of *The Faber Book of Modern Verse* (a pink paperback, 'Edited by Michael Roberts, revised by Anne Ridler'; the original 1936 edition printed 32 men and four women, and the 1965 edition printed 57 men and six women). I bought a number of the Penguin Modern Poets series that started in 1962 (77 men, four women) and Basil Bunting's *Briggflatts* from the Fulcrum Press (Lorine Niedecker the only woman on the list of 24 Fulcrum poets). The lack of women here was not conspicuous to me at the time because their absence was the norm. At my first boarding school there were just two women teachers, for English and 'handicrafts'; there was also the school matron and two or three much younger 'assistant matrons' who rarely – except for the one who married one of the Latin teachers – stayed long. At my second boarding school I don't recall a single woman teacher.

During the previous decades, the writers (and publishers) who had been producing the books I was avidly consuming were overwhelmingly not just male but class-bound, as D. J. Taylor notes (in *The Prose Factory: Literary Life in England since 1918*): 'the writers who populated the literary world of the interwar years tended to share similar backgrounds, to have attended the same kind of schools and universities (Oxford by far the most common destination) and to operate in the same kind of social landscapes'. When writers from other social backgrounds started arriving in the 1950s in significant numbers, these too were mostly male; a bunch of them got labelled the 'Angry Young Men'. For most of the literary establishment and even for many of the Angry Young Men, women's anger was still under wraps, and maybe if the wraps were kept tightly tied down it would just go away.

A chauvinistic take on *Robinson Crusoe*, a very selective obsession with the cultures of ancient Greece and Rome, and complete isolation from the opposite sex: at the posh end of the education system, this was a toxic mix. Long after the British Empire had crumbled, it was a recipe designed to perpetuate the racism, sexism and unearned entitlement upon which the empire had subsisted.[33] The motto of my secondary school was *Spartam nactus es, hanc exorna*: in the middle of the 20th century, in post-empire Britain, I was living in a militaristic city-state in ancient Greece.

On Fridays, marching around in battledress with rifles was compulsory.[34] On Sundays, attendance at both morning and evening services in the school chapel was also compulsory (except for God[35]). During the week the chaplain taught Divinity – which consisted of our reading aloud in class *The Man Born to be King*, the script of a 1940s radio drama series by Dorothy L. Sayers, daringly modern, resoundingly dull – and also European History, by which I mean we read a dog-eared textbook silently in class without making any significant progress towards page 704 while he did what? Marked our essays, slept, basked in his ineptitude. And he was a beater: if you annoyed him you were called up to the front, you bent over and he thrashed your arse with a cane,[36] putting into it every ounce of his self-hate. There was also, of course, a lot of running around and sport. The term generally used for all of this was 'Muscular Christianity', whose best-known proponent was Thomas Hughes, author of *Tom Brown's School Days* (1857): 'the least of the muscular Christians has hold of the old chivalrous and Christian belief, that a man's body is given him to be trained and brought into subjection,[37] and then used for the protection of the weak, the advancement of all righteous causes, and the subduing of the earth which God has given to the children of men.'

Haunting this environment were memories of war. At my first boarding school, Remembrance Day was as an important date in the calendar as Sports Day. All of our parents had lived through the 1939–45 war; even the names on the war memorials for those killed in the 1914–18 war were of men whom many people still alive had known, and loved. On Remembrance Day, war and boarding-school Christianity ('Onward, Christian soldiers') came together, and we remembered those who *gave their lives for their country* – which was presented, and still is, as the supreme example of 'doing the right thing'.[38] Remembrance Day mirrored Easter, but without the Resurrection. On the face of it, that at the same time we were reading the Wilfred Owen poem in which the line *'Dulce et decorum est pro patria mori'*is glossed as 'the old lie' was confusing; but children are accustomed from a very early age to dealing with contradictory reports on how the world works.

On Sunday, 4 October 1914, A. R. Smith, the headmaster of the public school I would attend in the 1960s, spoke to his pupils in the school chapel after they had returned from the long summer holiday: 'I do feel it is our duty to thank God for this war, as it is, here for us today. It has fallen to us at last to take up a cause which makes battle right and pure, purged from its grossness; for us renews the knightly vow of old, to defend the weak, to bring the power of the oppressor low . . . It would be a wretched thing indeed if, because you are back at school, you were to stand in any way apart from the great new fellowship, and the great new needs of empire today.' A forward-looking man – 'though trained in the Classics, he recognised the value of the Modern side, and, to meet this, insisted on the erection of new Science classrooms,' notes the school website – Smith is still blinded by the mist of righteousness in which the empire was wrapped. By May 1918 he has recognised that 'science has given to mankind undreamed-of powers of massacre' but is still, in January 1919, justifying sacrifice: 'This war, this victory was part of His work for the world, part of His suffering, part of His sacrifice, part of His Glory.'[39] In October 1919 he states that for the four previous years every single boy 'who had left the school fit to serve, had joined the army; more than half were killed or wounded'.

History, as I was taught it at school, ended with the 1914–18 war. A standard exam question required discussion of 'the causes of the First World War', and we dutifully read the books (by male historians) and wrote paragraphs about imperialist ambitions, balance-of-power alliances and the arms race. Polly Flint in Jane Gardam's *Crusoe's Daughter* (1968), told by a man who loves her in 1914 that he's going to war (but 'it won't last long'): 'Trying the word over, it sounded mad. Such a random thing. A boy with a gun in Bohemia, one afternoon. The lunatic world.' If I had simply suggested 'the lunatic world' – which included the educational system in which I was living – I'd have been given a detention and told to write the essay again, and again and again, until I got it right.

'In 1914 the whole youth of Europe, the simple children of simple people, were led out into a muddy place and commanded to slaughter one another.' That's Peter Levi in his funeral sermon for David Jones in 1974. During that war, around 2.5 million British men were conscripted into the army; these were lives taken, not given. More than 4 million non-European, non-white soldiers and auxiliaries also served in the 1914–18 war. They were led into that muddy place by men shaped and empowered by an education system based on male entitlement which during my schooldays was still in place, and to a dismaying extent still is. Clement Attlee (educated at Haileybury and Oxford) and Winston Churchill (Harrow and Sandhurst) were the prime ministers in the year I was born; then came Anthony Eden, Harold Macmillan and Alec Douglas-Home (all Eton and Oxford). Today, I'm not switching on the news in case I see Alexander Boris de Pfeffel Johnson or Jacob Rees-Mogg (Eton and Oxford, both). During most of my life the UK has been governed by politicians (men, almost without exception) whose assumptions were largely forged by a public-school ethos which was itself informed by the racism and misogyny and assumption of male entitlement of *Robinson Crusoe*. In 1979 half of the elected Members of Parliament were privately educated (in fee-paying schools, outside the state system); before that, more. In the parliament elected in June 2017, the number was down to 29 per cent[40] (including 45 per cent of Tory MPs and 15 per cent of Labour MPs), but that's still four times the percentage of privately educated people in the whole society. More than one in ten of the privately educated MPs went to Eton (still all boys; current fees, more than £40,500 per boy per year). So slowly, the numbers are changing, because a particular elite has held the stage and commanded the definitions of certain key words to power – security, patriotism, 'sovereignty' – for so long that their definitions have become the system itself.

Theodore Savage (1922) by Cicely Hamilton – who worked in military hospitals in France throughout the 1914–18 war and saw what happens when bombs are dropped from the air and poison gas is released – envisions an even greater cataclysm.[41] Theodore Savage is a civil servant who works 'without urgence, for limited hours, in a room that looked on Whitehall', and is knowledgeable about music and art ('his treasured Fragonard and his bell-toned Georgian wine-glasses'). He falls in love with his boss's daughter and, 'red to the ears and stammering platitudes', he asks her father's permission to marry her in, where else, the library, while daring to hope that this father will not 'insist upon too lengthy an engagement'. His timing is not good. The world's dominant political organisation, a kind of gentlemen's club of the wealthiest nations, miscalculates its response to a challenge to its authority, and war breaks out. This is war as enabled by the new technology: 'displacement of population, not victory in the field, became the real military objective'. Driven from the cities by aerial bombardment, starving millions roam the countryside, where crops and livestock are destroyed by chemical weapons. Within weeks, the structure of society – 'laws, systems, habits of body and mind' – has crumbled, 'leaving nothing but animal fear and the animal need to be fed'. 'Man, with bewildering rapidity, was slipping through the stages whereby, through the striving of long generations, he had raised himself from primitive barbarism.'

With survival now depending on brute force, women fare badly, and 'those women suffered most who had no man of their own to forage and fend for them, and were no longer young enough for other men to look on with pleasure'. One of these women, Ada, a former factory worker, attaches herself to Savage. The pair become a mocking echo of Crusoe and Friday (and Hamilton's exposition of their relationship is far more acute than the saccharine version of master-and-servant in Defoe's novel). Savage learns to fish and to snare birds and weave baskets; finding tools in abandoned houses, he improves his rough shelter and builds a clay oven. He treats Ada 'as a backward child', 'an encumbrance'; only after he returns one day from a foraging expedition with some women's clothes, which she delights in, does he become aware of her as a sexual being.

But they cannot enjoy each other as equals: Ada is 'flaccid, lazy, infantile of mind' and Savage cannot get beyond his awareness that Ada is 'so plainly his mental inferior'. Hamilton characterises Ada as 'one of the products of a mechanical civilisation; which, in saving her trouble, had stunted her'. Savage beats her ('she wriggled, plunged and howled'); she accepts the beating; she expects the beating. Only by physically acting out the power imbalance between them can they live together, forging a bond that accords with 'the barbaric institution of marriage' and its traditions 'of wifely obedience' (Cicely Hamilton, feminist and suffragist, was not a fan: see pages 55–7).

Savage and Ada, now pregnant, are absorbed into a ragged tribe of survivors bound together 'not by the love its members bore to each other, but by hatred and fear of the outsider'. Before he is accepted, Savage is questioned about his background. Because in this post-apocalypse world all links to the science and engineering that have enabled the Ruin are being cut – knowledge is being undone, a revenge upon 'progress' – Theodore Savage, educated at a public school and then Oxford, proficient in Latin and possessing impeccable good taste, is permitted to live only because in the pre-Ruin society he spent all his working life in admin, writing letters and reports and filing them, and has no specialist skills and is essentially useless.

3

Bad Sex

Defoe's Crusoe is two-dimensional: a simple chap stuck on an island,[42] a cardboard figure for every reader to project themself onto. (Walter de la Mare: 'that poor forked radish, a Man – with a thickish vigorous active headpiece, legs, hands, a Bible, a hatchet and a gun'.) And in Crusoe's 'eight and twenty years, two months, and 19 days' on his island sex is not on the menu.

Given that, in de la Mare's reckoning, 'Of all English writers Defoe was perhaps the furthest removed from the prig and the prude', Defoe's lack of interest in Crusoe as a sexual being is conspicuous. As announced on the title pages of two of his other novels, Moll Flanders was 'five times a wife (whereof once to her own brother)'; Colonel Jack was 'five times married to four whores'. But in *Robinson Crusoe*, women are excluded as strictly as from a boys' boarding school. During Crusoe's time on his island they simply don't exist, not even in his memory. When he returns to England he finds two sisters still alive – sisters who were never mentioned at the start of the novel, when Crusoe does mention his brothers – but they are neither described nor even named. Readers are informed of Crusoe's marriage and of the birth of his children and his wife's death in a single sentence. Eventually – in the penultimate paragraph of the novel – Crusoe sends a boat to maintain the embryo colony left behind on the island: 'and in it, besides other supplies, I sent seven women, being such as I found proper for service, or for wives to such as would take them'. Later, in *The Farther Adventures*, the colonists are gifted more women, and Crusoe approves their demeanour: 'all the five were most willing, quiet, passive and subjected creatures, rather like slaves than wives'.

For Crusoe himself, the lack of any sexual dimension to his experience appears not have been a problem; for his descendants, locked into the heredity, it has hugely messed things up. By denying Crusoe any sexual identity, Defoe infantilises him; in turn, Crusoe has infantilised his readers and followers.[43]

Not one of the Robinsons of Kafka, Céline, Spark or Keiller appears to enjoy any good sex – or to be capable of a mutually sustaining, loving relationship. And here is Enoch Robinson in Sherwood Anderson's *Winesburg, Ohio* (1919), who has come to New York to be an artist: 'Nothing ever turned out for Enoch Robinson. He could draw well enough and he had many odd delicate thoughts hidden away in his brain that might have expressed themselves through the brush of a painter, but he was always a child and that was a handicap to his worldly development. He never grew up and of course he couldn't understand people and he couldn't make people understand him. The child in him kept bumping against things, against actualities like money and sex and opinions.'

Robinson invites his artist friends to his room and 'They talk of art and are passionately, almost feverishly, in earnest about it. They think it matters much more than it does.' But their opinions about his own paintings dismay him: they cannot understand what he is trying to express. He dismisses them, and communes alone with imaginary friends.

He marries, gets a job, votes in an election and for a while has 'a newspaper thrown on his porch each morning'. But the marriage fails. He again populates his room with imaginary friends, 'made, I suppose, out of real people he had seen and who had for some obscure reason made an appeal to him. There was a woman with a sword in her hand, an old man with a long white beard who went about followed by a dog, a young girl whose stockings were always coming down and hanging over her shoe tops. There must have been two dozen of the shadow people, invented by the child-mind of Enoch Robinson, who lived in the room with him. And Enoch was happy. Into the room he went and locked the door.'

Except that the door cannot be locked. There's a woman: 'She saw me in the hallway of the house and we got acquainted.' She enters the room. 'She sat there in the room with me and she was too big for the room. I felt that she was driving everything else away. I was terribly afraid. I didn't want to let her come in when she knocked at the door but I couldn't sit still. "No, no," I said to myself, but I got up and opened the door just the same.'

It's a discomfiting tale of bad sex. Robinson: 'I wanted her all the time and I didn't want her.' He tells the woman about his imaginary people: 'I became mad to make her understand me and to know what a big thing I was in that room.' She *does* understand – 'and then all of a sudden things went to smash. A look came into her eyes and I knew she did understand. Maybe she had understood all the time. I was furious. I couldn't stand it.' He drives her out, 'and all the life there had been in the room followed her out'.

Early in the story the narrator mentions that Robinson's room is 'long and narrow, like a hallway', a little island, and 'It is important to get that fixed in your mind' because Robinson's story 'is in fact the story of a room almost more than it is the story of a man'.

Here is Robinson in Elizabeth Bowen's 'Summer Night', the final story in her 1941 collection *Look at All Those Roses*:

'Robinson did not frequent drawing rooms . . . When he was met, his imperturbable male personality stood out to the women unpleasingly, and stood out most of all in that married society in which women aspire to break the male in a man . . . When Robinson showed up, late, at the tennis club, his manner with women was easy and teasing, but abstract and perfectly automatic. From this had probably come the legend that he liked women "only in one way" . . . Robinson had on him the touch of some foreign sun.' Robinson is a 'factory manager'.[44] He has been settled in a small town in Ireland for three years, which sounds a reasonable length of time but in a small town isn't. He 'had at first been taken to be a bachelor' but he's not; he's living apart from his wife and children (three, one dead). Bowen's story is set on an evening in late summer during the Second World War ('Now that there's enough death to challenge being alive we're facing it that, anyhow, we don't live. We're confronted by the impossibility *of* living'); it includes three generations (including a child dancing naked on her parents' bed with snakes chalked on her skin), inconvenient guests, urgency and ennui. A married woman drives through the evening to spend the night with Robinson but when at last she is alone with him she is stranded by his stern imperturbability: 'The adventure (even, the pilgrimage) died at its root, in the childish part of her mind.' The only person who is at ease with Robinson is completely deaf: 'She does not hear with her ears, he does not hear with his mind. No wonder they can communicate.'

Here is Robinson addressing the narrator in Chris Petit's *Robinson*: 'I'm all in favour of the financial transaction myself. How many fucks, do you think, in the history of Soho?' They drink together in Soho and visit cinemas in which 'The actors went through the motions with an air of detachment, and the women, in the act of spreading themselves, appeared to retreat beyond reach into private reverie'; the narrator tells himself that Robinson's 'capacity for enormous violence was held in check only by my restraining presence'. Robinson has his own collection of films, among them one featuring an actor 'standing alone in the desert, naked except for a Stetson, deranged with booze and drugs, and masturbating while chanting to the camera: "Fuck you, Hollywood."' The narrator of the novel is a film editor,[45] and he and Robinson start making their own porn films to sell to a cable TV channel. They are joined by a group of 'outcasts of one sort or another, sexual and social, all losers' and a man named Cookie who 'played the minor public school, subaltern cad to perfection: the calculated drawl, the hint of a stammer, the insincere flattery, the saloon bar charm'. Soon, 'We had exhausted the lexicon of basic sexual gestures. Stefan fucks Lotte, so what? Robinson and I were both bored by our material.' Their films become more experimental – 'a montage of cut-up anatomies' – using strangers picked up on the streets. Fuelled by 'cocaine, uppers, downers, spirits, beer', Robinson treats the pick-ups, both male and female, 'with equal courtesy until frustration bred rage, and then he started to hit them'. Violence segues into torture. The narrator invents new scenarios: 'Robinson the neo-Nazi . . . Robinson the white slaver'. Robinson kills Cookie and the narrator films him walking back to his car: 'There was nothing to say. We had gone beyond words, had travelled too far together. These and other clichés filled my head.'[46]

In Graham Greene's *The Human Factor* (1978) Maurice Castle is a low-level member of the intelligence services working in an office in Mayfair. His black South African wife worries about their son going to a fee-paying prep school but Castle reassures her: 'He's a good runner. In England there's no trouble if you are good at any sort of games.' Games-playing is how Castle's colleagues think of their intelligence work: 'We are playing games, Daintry, games, all of us. It's important not to take a game too seriously or we may lose it.'

How important is it not to take games 'too seriously'? Seriously important. Careers and livelihoods depend upon just the right degree of non-seriousness. It's a British code and almost exclusively a male one. Women in *The Human Factor* are off to the side: secretaries, 'tarts', wives who are remote, girls in Raymond's Revuebar 'going through curious antics in a hammock'. A doctor working for the intelligence services declares: 'To tell you the truth I never had much interest in women. Don't mistake me – not in boys either. Now a good trout stream . . .' Another character: 'I like a good screw as much as the next man, but it's not all that important, is it?' Castle is in love with his wife, Sarah – a character essential to the book, which has to do with how love rather than ideology can be reason for betrayal – but even she is a blank, a cipher, her life barely imagined. Much whisky is drunk. Lunch at a shooting party consists of steak-and-kidney pudding followed by treacle tart, Stilton and port; at the Travellers Club, roast beef ('Perhaps a little overdone?'). The English stodginess is compounded, for most of the book, by the clunky, writing-by-numbers way the plot is advanced.

At the end of the novel Castle – whose interpretation of the rules of the game has been naïve – is alone, marooned in a bleak apartment in Moscow. During the day a 'large stout middle-aged woman', Russian, younger than Castle, comes to clean the apartment and treats him 'as if he were a child'. In the evenings 'he would warm some soup and sit huddled near the radiator, with the dusty disconnected telephone at his elbow, and read *Robinson Crusoe*'. Another marooned Englishman who has got his loyalties confused comes across Castle reading *Crusoe*: 'Ah ha, the great Daniel. He was one of us,' he announces, before producing 'a half bottle of whisky from the depths of his fur coat'. The other books available to Castle include 'school editions' of Shakespeare and a couple of Dickens novels; these school editions are what he grew up with (along with Rider Haggard: Allan Quatermain was his 'childhood hero'). Throughout Greene's novel, all the men playing the game of running the world and sworn to the Official Secrets Act are lonely and have difficulty in relating to others. Their education has been a disaster, for themselves and for everyone around them.

★

Writing about sex often involves – but doesn't have to – also writing about status, power and money.[46] Defoe was interested in all of these, and in the links between them. Walter de la Mare, noting Defoe's worldliness, remarks that he 'was fully as much interested in wives as in tradesmen' – an odd pairing, on the face of it, but a telling one. Defoe was himself a trades-man – at various times he sold wine, hosiery, woollen goods and tobacco; he owned a factory that made bricks and tiles; he bred civet cats for perfume; he invested in a diving bell to recover treasure from wrecked Spanish galleons; and he wrote extensively on the subject (*A General History of Trade*, 1713; *The Complete English Tradesman*, 1726). *Writing*, for Defoe, was a trade. Trade was how a man made his way in the world and, in this early capitalist society and for more than two centuries after, a woman too – although for the latter the almost exclu-sive means of advancement was founded upon surrender.

In *Marriage as a Trade* – published in 1909, in the same dec-ade that Thomas Godolphin Rooper was bleating about 'the dominion of the Anglo-Saxon' and a Cambridge University Press edition of *Robinson Crusoe* was celebrating Britain as 'the greatest colonizing power in the world' – Cicely Hamilton argues that for women denied access to both education and employment, marriage is the compulsory deal made for economic survival. She was writing mostly about middle-class women ('a class persistently set apart for the duties of sexual attraction, house-ordering and the bearing of children'), not factory workers like Ada in her novel *Theodore Savage* and not 'the prostitute class – a class which has pushed to its logical conclusion the principle that woman exists by virtue of a wage paid her in return for the possession of her person'. Hamilton was of her time (as I am of mine) in some of her assumptions: that women are more 'fastidious' in sex than men; that child-raising and fulfilment in work are incompatible. But she nailed it, the basic contract of marriage: 'essentially (from the woman's point of view) a commercial or trade undertaking'. Denied fulfilment of her own interests, it was demanded of a woman only 'that she should enkindle and satisfy the desire of the male, who would thereupon admit her to such share of the property he possessed or earned as should seem good to him. In other words, she exchanged, by the ordinary process of barter, possession of her person for the means of existence.'

Chapter by chapter, Hamilton explores the consequences of women being raised solely to become 'unintelligent breeding-machines' who are 'fed and lodged on the same principle a horse is fed and lodged – so that she may do her work, her cooking, her cleaning, her sewing, and the tending and rearing of her children'. None of those activities is more 'naturally' women's work than men's: 'woman, as we know her today,' Hamilton argues, 'is largely a manufactured product; the particular qualities which are supposed to be inherent in her and characteristic of her sex are often enough nothing more than the characteristics of a repressed class and the entirely artificial result of her surroundings and training.' The whole pattern is bizarre and illogical: women are trained for 'sex and motherhood' but about sex itself and the risk of STDs 'there exists a conspiracy of silence'; and the constrictions imposed upon women 'have defeated their own ends by discouraging the intelligence which ought to be a necessary qualification for motherhood, even if it is not a necessary qualification for wife-hood'. But power trumps logic, power *owns* logic: given 'the deep-rooted masculine conviction that [woman] exists not for her own benefit and advantage, but for the comfort and con-venience of man', then 'The masculine attitude in this matter seems quite logical.'

'One wonders,' writes Hamilton calmly but also with anger, 'what it has meant for the race – this persistent need of the man to despise his wife, this economic need of countless women to arrest their mental growth?' Nine years after *Marriage as a Trade* was published – and 199 years after the first publication of *Robinson Crusoe* – the right to vote in parliamentary elections in the UK was granted to women (aged over 30, and there were other limitations), but Hamilton's question has still not been addressed.

Cicely Hamilton's arguments were not new. Defoe voiced some of them himself through the character of Roxana in his 1724 novel named for her (but originally titled *The Fortunate Mistress*). 'One Morning, in the middle of our unlawful Free-doms, that is to say, when we were in Bed together', Roxana's lover asks her to marry him. She is pregnant by him; she loves him and will follow him to the East Indies, if that's where he wishes to go; but she refuses to marry him because 'the very Nature of the Marriage-Contract was, in short, nothing but giving up Liberty, Estate, Authority, and every-thing, to the Man, and the Woman was indeed, a meer Woman ever after, that is to say, a Slave'. She tells her lover that 'I had, perhaps, dif-fering Notions of Matrimony, from what the receiv'd Custom had given us of it; that I thought a Woman was a free agent, as well as a Man, and was born free, and cou'd she manage herself suitably, might enjoy that Liberty to as much Purpose as the Men do; that the laws of Matrimony were indeed, otherwise, and Mankind at this time, acted quite upon other principles; and those such, that a Woman gave herself entirely away from herself, in Marriage, and capitulated only to be, at best, an Upper-Servant'.

Roxana's lover is baffled: 'you go upon different notions from all the World; and tho' you reason upon it so strongly, that a Man knows hardly what to answer, yet I must own, there is something in it shocking to Nature, and something very unkind to yourself'. He is a decent and generous man; and when he leaves – 'for he cou'd not bear to see me, if he must not have me' – she pines for him. But she has been married before, has known 'this Thing call'd a Husband', and she is sticking to her principles. What sets Roxana apart from almost all other women is that as well as being 'beautiful, and agreeable, and not yet old' she is rich, and so can afford her principles. Arriving in London from the Netherlands, she rents a house near Charing Cross and takes on a coachman, a footman and three maids; 'and as for Jewels, I wanted none'.

Defoe was fascinated by Roxana, as he was by Moll Flanders – who remarks upon arriving in London that 'marriages were here the consequences of politic schemes for forming interests, and carrying on business, and that Love had no share, or but very little, in the matter'. In *An Essay upon Projects* (1697), published more than twenty years before he wrote *Crusoe*, Defoe had argued that women, 'with souls capable of the same accomplishments with men', surely hadn't been put into the world 'to be only stewards of our houses, cooks, and slaves'. He quoted a friend, 'a very fine woman': 'I had more need go to school than be married.' He proposed an 'Academy for Women' with colleges in every county of England and 'about ten for the city of London'; differing 'from all sorts of religious confinement, and, above all, from vows of celibacy', the Academy would offer women 'all the advantages of learning suitable to their genius'. The only reason for denying women a full education, he suggested, was 'fear they should vie with the men in their improvements'. When, late in life, he stumbled upon a new form of writing, prose fiction, it was inevitable that he should eventually choose to write about a woman who rises above the marriage trade and acquires as much power 'to entertain a Man, as a Man does a Mistress', and see how it played out.

In *Robinson Crusoe* Defoe denies himself this opportunity, and the novel is a dull thing because of it. But the link between sex and money is still there. In his early visits to the shipwreck to salvage tools, Crusoe comes across a drawer containing 'some European coin, some Brasil, some pieces of eight, some gold, some silver'. '"O drug!" said I aloud, "what are thou good for?"' Money is useless on the unpeopled island, and he's going to leave it 'to go to the bottom' – 'However, upon second thoughts, I took it away'. Those 'second thoughts': cautious Crusoe, keeping his options open. He wraps the money in canvas. Twenty-eight years later, leaving the island, he takes with him 'the great goat's-skin cap I had made, my umbrella, and my parrot; also I forgot not to take the money I formerly mention'd, which had lain by me so long useless . . .' One obvious reading of this might be: money as semen, as male ejaculate. Having no *useful* function on the island, semen – and by extension, any sexual self-awareness or feeling – has no role to play and can be stuck on a shelf to gather dust. Or, spelling it out a bit more: relations between men and women having been reduced to basic economics, with men holding all the power, sex for Crusoe on the island is an irrelevance (no one to trade with), but when he returns to society it's going to be back on the cards and he is careful not to neglect his canvas bag of testosterone and economic advantage.

In the single sentence near the end of *Robinson Crusoe* in which readers are informed of Crusoe's marriage, the birth of his children, the death of his wife and his renewed 'inclination to go abroad', Crusoe remarks that his marriage was 'not either to my disadvantage or dissatisfaction' – a canny trader speaking in double negatives, and not unhappy with his deal.[48]

★

As well as denying Crusoe a sexual identity, Defoe denies him self-doubt, which is another way of infantilising him. During his first year on the island Crusoe has a dream[49] in which a man descends 'from a great black cloud, in a bright flame of fire', approaches with a spear and declares: '"Seeing all these things have not brought thee to repentance, now thou shalt die."' Thereafter, he becomes pious: he has been wicked, he decides (though in what ways is not specified), and will now make up for it 'by a constant reading the scripture and praying to God', and this arrangement suits him well: 'Thus I liv'd mighty comfortably, my mind being entirely composed by resigning to the will of God, and throwing my self wholly upon the disposal of His providence.' He is still a worrier and still fearful for his safety, but his blind trust in God shuts off all radical introspection.

After Crusoe's discovery that cannibals are visiting the island, self-doubt does appear to creep in. At first, 'I could think of nothing but how I might destroy these monsters in their cruel bloody entertainment', and he finds a hollow tree in which he can hide and ambush the cannibals with his muskets and pistols; but then 'I began with cooler and calmer thoughts to consider what it was I was going to engage in; what authority or call I had, to pretend to be judge and executioner of these men as criminals, whom Heaven had thought fit for so many ages to suffer unpunish'd'. According to their own lights, the cannibals are not wrongdoers: 'They think it no more a crime to kill a captive taken in war, than we do to kill an ox; nor to eat human flesh, that we do to eat mutton.' Admirable relativism – but it derives from a very stage-managed self-questioning: first, Crusoe's consideration of the different lives of others does not extend to his own involvement in the slave trade; second, he is well aware that he is greatly outnumbered, and if just one cannibal escaped then 'they would come over again by thousands to revenge the death of their fellows, and I should only bring upon my self a certain destruction'. His conclusion – that 'it was not my business to meddle with them, unless they first attack'd me', and that his best course of action is 'by all possible means to conceal my self from them' – is founded in self-preservation.

Crusoe has a habit of tagging tedious little morals onto the end of each of his adventures; after his boat-building disaster, for example, he remarks on 'the folly of beginning a work before we count the cost, and before we judge rightly of our own strength to go through with it'. In *Serious Reflections During the Life and Surprising Adventures of Robinson Crusoe* (1720), Crusoe offers his more general afterthoughts[50] on 'the life of a man in an island' and concludes that 'life in general is, or ought to be, but one universal act of solitude'. It follows that 'The business is to get a retired soul, a frame of mind truly elevated above the world, and then we may be alone whenever we please, in the greatest apparent hurry of business or company.' As for sex, 'he that thinketh of a woman to desire her unlawfully has committed adultery with her already, though he has not looked on her, or has not seen her at that time' – so the whole thing is basically (a) 'unlawful', and (b) all about mental control, and is to be managed 'by bringing the mind to be above the power or reach of the allurement,[51] and to an absolute mastership over the wicked desire; otherwise the vicious desire remains, as the force remains in the gunpowder, and will exert itself whenever touched with the fire.'

To be a castaway is, I assume, a kind of living death. Crusoe could very easily go under; it would be the most natural thing in the world for him to do this: to curl up and die, or go crazy. Even Jane Gardam's Polly Flint, who hero-worships Crusoe, knows this: 'it is a sign of a human being's sanity, perhaps, that he should run mad in such circumstances, and perhaps Crusoe himself was insane when he arrived on the island, for his twenty-eight years in residence show only the growth of a most extraordinary and unnatural steadiness'. Walter de la Mare admires Defoe's novel for what it is, 'a triumph in its kind' – 'and yet one may pine for what, given a more creative imagination and a different Crusoe, the book might have been if the attempt had been made to reveal what a prolonged unbroken solitude, an absolute exile from fellow-creatures, and an incessant commerce with silence and the unknown, would mean at last to the spirit of man. A steadily debasing brutish stupidity? Hallucinations, extravagances, insanities, enravishment, strange guests?'

Defoe puts his man into an extreme situation and then reduces that situation to the kitchen sink; the black hole of isolation, of non-identity, is sketched in just sufficiently to provide a context for Crusoe's humdrum labours. Virginia Woolf: 'There are no sunsets and no sunrises; there is no solitude and no soul. There is, on the contrary, staring us full in the face nothing but a large earthenware pot.' The ultra-sensibleness of Crusoe, his sexlessness and his damping down of all strong emotion, are not *wrong* but they are beyond the normal range of what is normal.

★

In place of any kind of fulfilling sexual relationship, *Robinson Crusoe* posits male bonding. In his 2003 Nobel Prize lecture, 'He and His Man', Coetzee pairs Crusoe with Defoe, 'that dapper little man with the quick step and the mole upon his chin',[52] and asks: 'How are they to be figured, this man and he? As master and slave? As brothers, twin brothers? As comrades in arms? Or as enemies, foes?' Other possibilities: as straight man and stooge? Main man and sidekick? Good cop and bad cop?

Probably the most common figuration of male duos in literature – I haven't done a statistical survey – is master-and-servant, if included are those bondings in which the roles are not explicit but definitely there: Don Quixote and Sancho Panza, Diderot's Jacques and his servant, Bertie Wooster and Jeeves, obviously, but also Sherlock Holmes and Dr Watson (and, perhaps, Dr Johnson and Boswell and any number of male writers and their 'amanuenses'). Squires, valets, manservants: from long before Crusoe until only a couple of generations ago, the Western class and economic structures provided for – *required* – this tight little bond between a man (of a certain class) and his man that might often be more intimate, without necessarily being sexual – more intimate *because* non-sexual – than that between a man and his wife. The fagging system at English public schools was specifically designed to prepare posh boys for this master–servant relationship.

Masters-and-servants reflected in miniature a power structure based on class. Compounding the imbalance in physical strength between men and women, that same power structure was, and still is, a determining factor in relations between the sexes. For a glimpse into how power in the 18th century was *lived*, here is the very first entry (8 February 1709) in the diary kept by William Byrd – a Fellow of the Royal Society, owner of a library of more than 4,000 books and of tobacco plantations in Virginia: 'I rose at 5 o'clock this morning and read a chapter in Hebrew and 200 verses in Homer's *Odyssey*. I ate milk for breakfast. Jenny and Eugene were whipped. I danced my dance. I read law in the morning and Italian in the afternoon.' (Jenny and Eugene were household slaves. As for 'danced my dance', a phrase which recurs very frequently in the diaries, I don't know, and the editors of Byrd's diaries don't speculate, but I assume wanking.) From 1717 to 1719 Byrd lived in London; here are diary extracts from April 1719, the month when *Robinson Crusoe* was first published:

13 April: About 6 o'clock I went to Mrs U-m-s but they were from home; then to Lady Powlett's but she was asleep; then to Will's where I read the news; then to Lady Guise's till nine and then to Ozinda's where I drank a dish of chocolate, and then went to Court. When I came home my man was asleep and I beat him. I said my prayers.

14 April: I wrote a letter to Mrs B-s to refuse to lend her fifty pounds. [. . .] About 10 o'clock went with Mrs S-t-r-d to the bagnio and rogered her once.

23 April: I rose about 7 o'clock and read a chapter in Hebrew and some Greek in Lucian. [. . .] Then was I carried by a woman I met in the street to a pretty Frenchwoman with whom I supped and gave her some chicken and asparagus but did not roger her. About twelve I went home and neglected my prayers.

27 April: I went to Mrs B-r-n where I drank three dishes of chocolate and then went to court and talked abundantly to Mrs Howard. In coming home I took a woman into the coach and committed uncleanness and then went home and said my prayers. [53]

30 April: Then we went to Kensington Garden where we talked till 8 o'clock and then returned and I went to see my French whore where I supped and ate some fricassee of chicken. I gave the whore two guineas and committed uncleanness and then went home in the chair and said my prayers.

Robinson Crusoe and Friday are master and servant, with the white man having all the power, and Defoe's account of their relationship is patronising and sentimental: 'I began really to love the creature; and on his side, I believe he lov'd me more than it was it was possible for him to love any thing before.' See back to page 47 for a far more searching take on a bonding in which one of the pair holds all the power.

Beyond the master-and-servant template, other examples of literary male duos include:[54] Robinson (Kafka's) and Delamarche; Robinson (Céline's) and Bardamu; Robinson (Keiller's) and the Narrator, and Robinson (Petit's) and *his* narrator; Flaubert's Bouvard and Pécuchet; Beckett's Mercier and Camier, and then Vladimir and Estragon in *Waiting for Godot*; James Kennaway's Link and Dr Fiddes;[55] W and Lars in Lars Iyer's *Spurious* (and then *Dogma* and *Exodus*). The authors of all of these books are male.[56] The majority of the male-duo relationships are written in the comic vein – which, in the master-and-servant category, allows for the reversal of the power balance for comic or satirical effect but no structural change.

In Flaubert's *Bouvard and Pécuchet* (1881), Crusoe's earnest labours on his island are spun through a hall of mirrors and emerge as high comedy. By trial and error, Crusoe did at least manage to get his fences to stay upright and his barley to grow and his pots to hold water. Bouvard and Pécuchet, a pair of copy-clerks who retire to a farm in the countryside, have the latest scientific knowledge and research available to them, yet everything they attempt – in gardening, agriculture, food preservation, chemistry and medicine, as well as the more abstract fields – turns out disastrously. Their seedlings wash away, their wheat stinks, their sheep drop dead and also their oxen ('a consequence of Bouvard's phlebotomies'), their beer gives everyone cramps, their haystacks catch fire, their pond drains dry, their preserves rot, their bottles of wine explode, their medicines make the patients more ill, their attempts to mate a ram with a lamb (and a duck with a hen, a dog with a sow) come to nothing, their tapping for fossils collapses a cliff, their carefully restored Renaissance chest is destroyed by a runaway cow, their study of aesthetics gives them jaundice, their attempts at love end in rejection and disease, their gymnastics leave them sore and bleeding, their reading of philosophy leads only to 'the certainty that nothing exists'. They research suicide and fail to kill themselves; they find a doctor's letter reassuring the local magistrate that they are not criminally insane – they've not been *radicalised* – but merely a couple of harmless idiots.

'What's the point of all this?' 'Maybe there is no point.'

In Lars Iyer's *Spurious* (2011),[57] W and Lars are two low-level academics, one in the south-west of England and the other in the north-east. Lars lives in an apartment that's assailed by an apocalyptic damp (it's 'off the scale'; the professionals shake their heads and mutter that they've 'never seen anything like it'). They bicker, tease, read books they don't understand and drink neat gin. Briefly, they wonder which of them is Kafka and which Brod, before agreeing that they are both Brod. Canada, 'with its pristine blue lakes and bear-filled wilderness' and its different kind of cold ('not a wet cold like over here') is the place to go to, a place where one could be 'a different kind of man', and Lars writes references for W ('the finest thinker of his generation') and they hear nothing back, the Canadians are 'remote as Martians'. Their joint acceptance that they are living in End Times – and that any belief that salvation might lie in *books* is a joke – goes to their heads at least as much as the gin: 'I am his idiot, but he is mine, and it's this we share in our joy and our laughter, as we wake each day into the morning of our idiocy, wiping the sleep from our eyes and stretching.'

On the other side of − or underneath − Exquisite Doom is Hilarious Doom. If the comedy here is black it's not matt black, it's glossy, even fluorescent: lurid, twitchy (odd spasms of hope still flickering uselessly, 'like the animals who come out of their burrows after winter, shivering but excited'), jerky − and now that I've written that word I think of Punch and Judy shows, the way the puppets bash each other flat and then spring up and go through it all again and again and again. *Spurious* is threaded through with a crazy End Times glee, the glee that you feel when your team, which you do genuinely support, is losing five−nil and a balance is tipped, no way back now, and you decide that if they're going to fail then let them at least fail spectacularly, with abject abandon, pile it on.

Within all the books in which the male duos appear, the sexuality, and more specifically the men's relationship with women, is uneasy and confused. More bluntly: there's a recurrent streak of misogyny. Bouvard and Pécuchet, joshing along in their very first chat, agree that women are 'frivolous, shrewish, and stubborn', and that 'you were better off living without them'. Attempting a seduction, Pécuchet's 'desire was made all the keener by his fear of satisfying it'. Beckett's Mercier is married but regrets it: 'The mother of my children. Mine own. Inalienable. Toffana. You never met her. She lives on. A tundish. Like fucking a quag. To think it was for this hectolitre of excrement I renegued my dearest dream.' Also in *Mercier and Camier* is Mr Conaire: 'Forgive me, he said, when I think of women I think of maidens, I can't help it. They have no hairs, they pee not neither do they cack.' In *Spurious*, W's wife has 'complete contempt' for him, which makes him happy: 'That's how it should be. Your partner should always have contempt for you.'

I could hardly be less interested in whether these male two-somes are gay and/or are having some good sex elsewhere. I'm just reading what's on the page, and what does interest is that the (male) writers – and Defoe too – have chosen to structure their books around characters who are unable as couples to make children. That's no bar to sexual intimacy, but this too is largely excluded. The nearest Bouvard and Pécuchet get is their hydrotherapy sessions, viewed by 'scandalised' locals: 'The two men, naked as savages, splashed each other with water, then scurried back into their rooms.' Mercier and Camier, staying overnight with their friend Helen, are offered her bed or a couch. Mercier declares 'I'll sleep with none'; Camier is interested in 'a nice little suck-off' but Helen is not. On a second visit they do enjoy languid sex – 'in the twofold light of lamp and leaden day, they squirmed gently on the carpet, their naked bodies mingled, fingering and fondling' – but next day they are back on the streets.

Admitting good sex – and certainly family – into the books would have tipped them into different directions and made them not the books the authors set out to write; but there is still a Puritanism here that goes back to *Crusoe*. With sex off the menu, or offered only as an extra along with *frites*, what's left is mostly ideas, friendship, and running for the bus. These are plenty to be going along with, but you can't *live* off them. In the case of *Spurious*, it's as if non-procreation were as much a given as climate catastrophe and economic implosion; or as if there were some causal link between them.

The male twosomes are parodies of marriage (or, as parodies sometimes are, a more accurate representation of the thing than the clichés offered by the media). They don't so much rub along as up against each other; they don't so much go from A to B as round in circles; and it's this *not going anywhere* that makes them essentially comic.

Comedy – deep comedy – is pain and recognition. Comedy is more generous than tragedy; it can include tragedy in a way that isn't usually reciprocated. But comedy can also be a cop-out: turning things that are difficult to deal with into banter, making a virtue of its own embarrassment and a whole career out of this. Modern literature is rife with well-written bad sex; notoriously, good sex is harder to write. It doesn't help that the book widely considered to be the first English novel, *the* precedent, simply turns a blind eye to the whole subject.

★

The umbrella of Mercier and Camier is a stunted little thing, more of a child's parasol, a comic add-on like Charlie Chaplin's bendy cane. They can't get it up (they have erectile dysfunction?), nor even decide *when* to put it up: now, or wait till the rain is even worse? It is comic not least because, as Robert Louis Stevenson suggests in his essay on 'The Philosophy of Umbrellas',[58] an umbrella is a 'sacred symbol of domestic virtues', and those are virtues that Mercier and Camier conspicuously lack. Stevenson: 'A ribbon of the Legion of Honour may prove a person's courage; a title may prove his birth; a professorial chair his study and acquirement; but it is his habitual carriage of the umbrella that is the stamp of Respectability.' The umbrella of Robinson Crusoe is painstakingly made and highly effective – it 'kept off the sun so effectually that I could walk out in the hottest of the weather with greater advantage than I could before in the coolest, and when I had no need of it, I could close it, and carry it under my arm' – but did he really *need* it? Stevenson suggests that 'surely one who had borne the hard labour of a seaman under the tropics for all these years could have supported an excursion after goats or a peaceful *constitutional* arm in arm with the nude Friday' without worrying about the sun: 'No, it was not this: the memory of a vanished respectability called for some outward manifestation, and the result was – an umbrella.'

Crusoe is not intended to be comic in any way and, even after the arrival of Friday, was never about couples or coupling. *Crusoe* comes out of Protestantism, which is about – in contrast to family-oriented Catholicism – the individual relating one-to-one with the godhead. *Crusoe* was about solitariness; more specifically, male solitariness: men not talking, not 'opening up'; men and their sheds; men and their hobbies (model railways, stamp collections, bird-watching, angling); men and their thing about *lighthouses*, and climbing mountains and disappearing into jungles; men with their stiff upper lips and their campaign medals;[59] men refusing to go to the doctor; men obsessed by numbers, statistics, performance; men and sport, men and maps, men and guns, men and pornography, men and their *kit* and men with their knowingness about machines and gadgets but hardly ever about their own bodies. You know: men – and their fear of losing face, their determination to appear *respectable* whatever the circumstances.

Defoe's *Robinson Crusoe* didn't just license, it mainstreamed this masculine essence. It also reinforced the male monopoly over certain activities and fields of knowledge – exploration and physical adventure; science and engineering; tools and how to use them – which women were neither expected nor permitted to be interested in. Not entirely Defoe's fault, of course; more responsible are those who made a role model of a character whose author, by isolating him from human society, could not have placed him in a more unnatural, artificial environment.[60] What then became normalised is the essence of shipwrecked men, *damaged* men. And thereby, because of the power wielded by men, damaged women.

★

The first coffee house in London was opened in 1652, and by the beginning of the next century there were several hundred. They became popular places for men to discuss the ways of the world; women were largely excluded.[59] The economy was complicated, as always: some coffee houses were owned, and hosted, by women; on the other hand, women who wandered into the coffee houses to sell things might be assumed to be selling also themselves. The coffee houses were the forerunners of gentlemen's clubs (a number of which, in London in 2019, still exclude women from membership). Defoe knew these places well. He is reputed to have met Alexander Selkirk, the possible inspiration for Robinson Crusoe, in a coffee house in Bristol.

For generations, not only were women shut out from positions and places of power, both formal and informal, but the terms and conditions of female solitariness were largely set by men. I'm thinking here of my mother's Crusoe period, her nearly fifty years of living alone as a widow; and of Polly Flint in Jane Gardam's *Crusoe's Daughter*.[62] Polly's period of, in effect, widowhood lasts even longer than my mother's. The man people assume she is going to marry is killed in the First World War; the man she loves marries another, and then another. Though maybe neither of those men would have done; she reckons marriage very quickly becomes a habit, like religion.

An orphan, Polly Flint is brought up by two aunts in a bleak house on the coast of north-east England. Solitary and bookish, she adopts Crusoe as a father figure while being well aware that his limitations are a strong part of his appeal: 'Crusoe was so sensible. And so unimaginative. He sorts you out. I love him.' Instinctively, she is drawn to his lack of frills: 'not a lot of gush or romantic love'. By the time, in her teens, that Polly Flint finds herself having to defend *Robinson Crusoe* against the accusation that it contains 'no trace, no *trace* of poetry', she has read it twenty-three times. She understands that her trouble in life 'is perhaps that I am a girl'; had she been 'some stubborn boy perhaps called Jack or Harry' she would have been sent away to school, but as it is she is locked into caring for the ageing aunts and 'all hope for me is that someone will come and marry me to make things complete and take me away'. She is marooned both in the big yellow house by the sea and in her gender, and the attraction of Crusoe is clear: 'He didn't go mad. He was *brave*. He was wonderful. He was like women have to be almost always, on an island. Imprisoned. The only way to survive it is to say it's God's will.'

Of course Crusoe cannot save Polly Flint. His wonderfulness is impossible to live up to. She envies him 'his sensible sexlessness which he seemed so easily to have achieved'. ('He was a man of course, so it would be easier. He didn't have blood pouring out of himself every four weeks until he was old.') Nor can the real men whom Polly knows – 'cautious, inadequate, shadowy, grasping, dull' – live up to him. After the First World War – Polly is still only twenty in 1918 – she spends years obsessively translating *Robinson Crusoe* into German and French and then writing an unfinishable book on *Crusoe* as a form of spiritual biography, subsiding into alcoholism as she does so. She is saved, eventually, not by a book but by work (as Crusoe saved himself), after her servant forces her back into the social world as a teacher. At the end of her long life she announces, 'I'm over fiction', and remarks – in conversation with the ghost of Crusoe – that 'quite often people confuse their fictional heroes with God. As they confuse their human lovers. Or themselves. It is a great hindrance to a happy life.'

'If only he had been a woman!' – that's Crusoe in Elizabeth Bishop's 'Crusoe in England'[63] recalling the arrival of Friday on his island: 'He'd pet the baby goats sometimes, / and race with them, and carry one around. / – Pretty to watch; he had a pretty body'. The marooned Crusoe had plenty of time for idle speculation, for turning over in his mind any number of what-if questions and if-only fantasies. What if Friday really had been a woman (but given Crusoe's sense of entitlement, she might not have had much enjoyment). What if Crusoe himself had been a woman,[64] or been *written* by a woman. What if women had been welcomed on equal terms with men into the coffee houses of 18th-century London. What if the half of the human species that is physically stronger than the other half had not determined that the role of the other half was to be 'proper for service'. What if rats had destroyed Crusoe's corn and his ammunition had run out. What if, following the dream that turned Crusoe pious and God-fearing, he had had a second dream that told him to ignore the previous, it had been sent in error. What if Crusoe could turn himself into a goat: at least *they* seemed to be having some fun.

4

Migrants, Vagrants, Englishmen

The print of a naked foot discovered by Crusoe along the shore of his island – the most widely illustrated footprint in all of British literature – is that of a migrant.

Just *one* print? Coming from nowhere, leading nowhere?

Crusoe is 'terrify'd to the last degree'. He thinks at first that it's the work of the Devil – but the Devil wouldn't be so stupid as to leave his mark in a place where the odds against Crusoe finding it were ten thousand to one, and it would soon be washed away by the sea. He concludes 'that it must be some of the savages of the main land over against me, who had wander'd out to sea in their canoes, and either driven by the currents, or by contrary winds, had made the island'.

After an initial period of confusion – 'what course to take for my security I knew not' – Crusoe reinforces his stockade,[65] adding an outer wall 'thicken'd with pieces of timber, old cables, and everything I could think of to make it strong'. From the wreck of the ship which brought him to the island he retrieves more muskets, and places these in frames in the outer wall, 'so I could fire all the seven guns in two minutes time: This wall I was many a weary month finishing, and yet never thought my self safe till it was done.'

Walls are a Crusoe obsession: he devotes more time and ingenuity to them than is justified by a simple desire for 'security from ravenous creatures, whether men or beasts'. Soon after his arrival on the island he builds a fence with stakes and cables on ground sheltered by a steep rock, and 'into this fence or fortress, with infinite labour I carry'd all my riches'. Then he erects a second wall of turf outside the first and hollows out a cave in the rock. Entrance to his dwelling is not by a gate but a ladder, so that 'nothing could come at me from without, unless it could first mount my wall'. After an earth tremor causes part of the roof of his cave to collapse, he considers starting all over again in a more open place, but just the thought of this is exhausting. Instead, in another part of the island, he builds a sort of holiday home, his 'bower', surrounded 'with a strong fence, being a double hedge, as high as I could reach, well stak'd, and fill'd between with brushwood'. After he rescues Friday, he solves the problem of 'where I should lodge him' by making a wooden door to his own sleeping area: 'I barr'd it up in the night, taking in my ladders too; so that Friday could no way come at me in the inside of my innermost wall, without making so much noise in getting over, that it must needs waken me.' He adds 'a kind of trap-door, which if it had been attempted from the outside, would not have open'd at all, but would have fallen down and made a great noise; and as to weapons, I took them all into my side every night'.

Crusoe's fixation on his new wall follows from his belief that any people from 'the main land' visiting his island must be 'savages' and 'against me'. That the visitors turn out to be cannibals – and not Christians, and they probably don't wash their hands before meals either – doesn't so much legitimise his racist assumptions as embody them. Defoe's portrayal of all the non-white people in *Robinson Crusoe* as cannibals[66] is akin to a 21st-century British novelist portraying all the Muslim characters in their novel as terrorists.

Defoe's Robinson Crusoe is himself as much an immigrant on the island as Friday, and in England was born to an immigrant father: his family name is an English corruption (a big one: the two names don't even sound alike)[67] of the German Kreutznaer, 'my father being a foreigner of Bremen'. Kafka's Robinson, an immigrant in America, is said to be Irish (though the head waiter at the Hotel Occidental doesn't believe this: 'no Irishman in that country's history has ever been called Robinson'). Céline's Robinson is French. Weldon Kees's Robinson is American. Spark's Robinson was born in Gibraltar and educated in France and England and then in an Irish seminary. Chris Petit's Robinson is not straightforwardly English, more 'like some foreigner imitating what he thinks is the English way'. The nationality of Keiller's Robinson is obscure: 'Of course, Robinson wasn't his real name, and he wasn't English. He had arrived in London in 1966, from Berlin, before which his history was uncertain.'

The title of Defoe's satirical poem *The True-Born Englishman* (1701), written to defend the Dutch-born King William against xenophobic attacks, was ironic. Defoe was fully aware that, as he wrote in 'An Explanatory Preface', 'speaking of Englishmen *ab origine*, we are really all foreigners ourselves':

> Thus from a mixture of all kinds began,
> That het'rogeneous thing, an Englishman:
> In eager rapes, and furious lust begot,
> Betwixt a painted Britain and a Scot.
> Whose gend'ring off-spring quickly learn'd to bow,
> And yoke their heifers to the Roman plough:
> From whence a mongrel half-bred race there came,
> With neither name, nor nation, speech nor fame.
> In whose hot veins new mixtures quickly ran,
> Infus'd betwixt a Saxon and a Dane.
> [. . .]

> The wonder which remains is at our pride,
> To value that which all wise men deride.
> For Englishmen to boast of generation,
> Cancels their knowledge, and lampoons the nation.
> A true-born Englishman's a contradiction,
> In speech an irony, in fact a fiction.

Defoe's Crusoe, nevertheless, offspring of an English writer (who Frenched-up his name) and roped into an education system designed to produce the administrating class of the British Empire and maintained long beyond that empire's end, came to be perceived as a representative Englishman (Frederick Brereton, in his introduction to my 1953 edition of *Robinson Crusoe*, is especially keen on Crusoe's 'typically Anglo-Saxon stolidity'). No one more adamantly Christian than a born-again one; no fighter-for-the-cause more fanatic than a fresh recruit; no one more English, sometimes, than an assimilated immigrant, their status and recognition won by such hard labour. Out of this *manufactured* identity grew Crusoe's sense of embattlement, the obverse of his sense of entitlement (the two often go together, like triumphalism and defensiveness, or paranoia): the walls, the trapdoor, the fear of strangers (and women).

The wayward lives of Crusoe's descendants are a demonstration of how quickly a manufactured identity can unravel. In addition, happening to be white, male, and therefore implicated in the oppressive history of old-man Crusoe – in no particular order: wealth amassed from slavery, empires carved out by gunpowder, male repression of women – the 20th-century Robinsons find themselves in an out-of-kilter world in which they can neither embrace their privilege nor disown it, so in limbo.

★

In Kafka's *Amerika* Karl Rossmann, after being thrown against a cupboard in a fight with Delamarche and Robinson in the apartment where they are all living with Brunelda, wakes in the night and tries to find the light switch to see how badly he's been hurt. Groping along the floor, he comes across a boot, and then a leg: 'That had to be Robinson, who else would sleep in his boots?'

The Robinsons of Kafka, Céline and Keiller are all of no fixed abode. Kafka's Robinson and Céline's pick up casual work when they need and are able to; Keiller's Robinson relies on part-time teaching to fund his amateur research into the matter of England, and the end result is cans of film in a caravan in a field. Their natural habitat is the road; whether moving towards something (money, knowledge, love) or away (from *administration*) is largely irrelevant. Rejecting the Crusoe idea of settlement – which was never really *his* idea: his island huts and walls were an enforced holiday, admittedly a long one, from a life 'possest with a wandring spirit' – they have reverted to a life of drifting. Of course Robinson sleeps in his boots, the mud caking hard in the night – they'd get nicked if he didn't. Boots are the emblem of Robinson, as they are of Estragon in *Waiting for Godot* – those badly fitting boots which he leaves on the ground at the end of the first Act and which are still there at the start of the second, though now he doesn't recognise them as his.

Rimbaud, hero of Keiller's Robinson, was also of no fixed abode; and though much of his short life is well documented there are periods, even during his stays in England when he was watched by the police, when he contrived to wander off the radar. Scotland? Scarborough? In his poem 'Ma Bohème' he writes of his 'wounded' boots: 'Comme des lyres, je tirais les élastiques / De mes souliers blessés'. In northern France and in Abyssinia, Rimbaud tramped many hundreds of miles.

When, towards the end, his leg was amputated in Marseilles, he surely knew the game was up.

In 1998 Paul Scofield, who narrated Patrick Keiller's first two *Robinson* films, sent Keiller a postcard of a photograph by August Sander[68] titled *Landstreicher* – in English, sometimes *Itinerants*, sometimes *Vagrants*, which carries not quite the same meaning. Keiller thought the figure on the left looked like Scofield, and the figure on the right might resemble Robinson ('More recently, I have imagined he might look quite different'). Dated 1929, the photograph is from the part of Sander's encyclopedic series *People of the 20th Century* that also includes photographs titled *Vagabonds*, *Tramps*, *Gypsies*, *Unemployed* and *Casual Labourer*.

Take the photograph back fifteen years and it could be of Kafka's Delamarche and Robinson on the road to Butterford, 'where it was rumoured that work was to be had'. In the 1920s, Sander's itinerants were two of many hundreds of thousands on the roads of Europe and the US, and they are nameless. Harold Owen (Wilfred's brother), back in England in 1919 after serving in the navy during the 1914–18 war and needing work, was 'sick to death of this England who smugly looked on while her young men just out of the War peddled bootlaces and collar studs or lined up in their scores for the chance to sell goods . . .' Joseph Roth describes a hostel for the homeless in Berlin in 1920: 'Many are footsore. Some of these people have walked all their lives . . . The provisional or the contingent has become their normal way of life, and they are at home – in their homelessness.' Most seasonal work on the land and much casual work in factories were done by itinerants; it's how national economies got by, and in the richer bits of Europe still do. John Berger's 1975 *A Seventh Man* was titled for the migrant workers who made up one in seven of the manual workforce in Germany and Britain (and a larger proportion in some other European counties); in May 2016 the *Guardian* reported that 'foreign national migrants working in Britain account for 10.6% of the workforce'.

Sander's itinerants are sturdy, unbowed, resilient. But any romance of the open road that they might be felt to illustrate is an illusion exclusive to the viewer. Until they bump up against a political border or reach a farm or factory that's hiring and are lined up in a queue and registered, itinerants (vagrants, tramps, vagabonds, migrants) evade administration, but the only real freedom they have is the freedom to disappear. Bodies are found in ditches or are washed up on beaches and counted, and thereby enter the realm of statistics, but the true number of migrants who have died or who have been sold into slavery while on the road, or the sea, is unknowable.

According to the writer Sam Cooper, 'The shift that has taken place in the Robinson character from Kafka and Céline to Kees and Petit is that, in the former, Robinson is just about able to eke out an existence at the peripheries of society; in the latter, more recent texts, he is not, and he is forced to disappear. Robinson finds himself adrift from a society that has become increasingly administered.' [69] Further: the 'spectrality' of Keiller's Robinson 'reflects the asynchronicity between the historical possibilities that he attempts to keep alive and the fallen present/bleak future of global capitalism'.

To be administered – postcoded, credit-checked, means-tested, taken off one list and added to another – is itself a way of being vanished. To be accounted for is not the same as being taken account of. Someone who is reckoned only as a consumer, whether of services or goods, and defined by a monetary value, is invisible.

Kafka's Robinson fades out (the novel is unfinished). Céline's Robinson is shot dead in a taxi. Keiller's Robinson vanishes, leaving behind just a few cans of film. The most provocative act of Muriel Spark's Robinson is his deliberate disappearance (which prompts the other characters to suspect one another of his murder); replying to Spark's narrator, who is infuriated after his return by his refusal to give any explanation for his behaviour, Robinson says, 'Yours, of course, is the obvious view. Well, my actions are beyond the obvious range. It surely needs only that you should realise this, not that you should understand my actions.' Weldon Kees's Robinson [70] is just plain AWOL, his whole point.

Petit's Robinson carries 'no watch, no address book, no scraps of paper, no cheque books, no credit cards, none of the junk or bits of identification that most people accumulate': 'Robinson was there, all right, a character, but all the little things about him − the lack of identification, the use of cash − suggested someone outside everything.' Asked by Robinson why he is looking at him, the narrator replies: 'I told him I'd decided he didn't exist. He threw back his head and laughed. "Who does, old man? Who does?"'

Petit's novel *Robinson* bends towards apocalypse: floods, rats, destitution, 'psychic brutality'. A woman falls to her death from the roof of the porn factory in a tropical storm, and the adjacent shanty town becomes 'a sea of mud'. London is paralysed by freak weather: 'As the fog closed in, there came a strange screeching, like clouds were scratching the buildings as they enveloped them.' Public transport shuts down, electricity is cut off. The narrator edits random sequences into Robinson's unfinished, unfinishable film ('A moving walkway at Gatwick airport; tank manoeuvres in the desert'), and closes in hallucination: 'the whole raft of Soho breaking from the rest of the city, and the smoke and the fire'.

Towards the end of Keiller's film *London*, in which Robinson attempts but fails to get a handle on the city's 'problem', the narrator announces: 'The true identity of London is in its absence. In this alone it is truly modern. London was the first metropolis to disappear.'[71]

★

Seated at a café table with Robinson on an April afternoon and watching the traffic slide by, the shoppers shopping, the joggers jogging, the beggars begging, the lovers loving, the drinkers drinking, the lobbyists lobbying and the property developers developing and the bankers banking (but I can't actually *see* much of this) and the walkers walking at the regular bipedular pace, give or take, which through the eyes of a child in the back of a car can seem infinitely sinister, I'd like to discuss with Robinson this: why are there not *more* crazy people running amok with machetes or second-hand Kalashnikovs?

He doesn't have to answer. Robinson is, you understand, a fictional character – or not even that, more a sort of ghost. The waitress is looking at him as if she suspects he is about to pocket the teaspoons.

On his tight little island, Crusoe was king: 'My island was now peopled, and I thought myself very rich in subjects; and it was a merry reflection which I frequently made, how like a king I look'd.' Adopted as an unofficial national myth and promulgated in schools during the period of British imperial expansion, *Robinson Crusoe* promised dominion in return for hard work and trust in God. The obvious problem here is that there cannot be kings without subjects, and for most of those doing the work and the trusting in God – even those lucky enough to be born white and male and in the rich West – the promise of dominion is not fulfillable, and never was. Crusoe had an empty island and a head start over the handful of others who arrived and became his 'subjects'; at the start of 2019 the population of the UK is around 67 million. The basic Crusoe formula dooms most of those who are encouraged to sign up to it – encouraged by those who already have dominion, often by inheritance, and who aren't in a hurry to give it up – to failure and exclusion.

Robinson was one of 425 workers who lost their jobs when Samsung closed its electronics factory in Billingham in January 2004 – the same factory whose opening by the Queen in 1995, following a commitment from the UK government to grants of £58 million plus another £13 million as an interest-free loan, featured in Patrick Keiller's film *Robinson in Space*. Samsung, which made record profits in the final quarter of the previous year ($2 billion), blamed high UK wages ('£4.50 to £5.50 per hour') compared those in China (50p) and Slovakia (£1). Many of those who lost their jobs lived in the constituency of Prime Minister Tony Blair, who commented: 'This is part of the world economy in which we live.'[72]

Robinson has worked as a shelf stacker, bottle washer, fruit picker, fish gutter, turkey plucker, shoeshiner, baggage handler, toilet cleaner, street sweeper, cold-caller, dog walker, hod carrier and gravedigger, all for the minimum wage or less. Robinson's mother believed that he should be able make a fortune on the stock market, if everyone else can do it why not him. Robinson has been invited to receive many millions of dollars from Nigerian bank accounts. Robinson has some 1952 coronation memorabilia in a drawer – a mug, a medal, a teaspoon – which his uncle said would one day be worth a lot of money but when he takes them to the pawnbroker the guy just shakes his head.

What happens when you've put in all the hard work and still can't afford the rent on a place to live? When you've been brought up to believe that your country is superior to others and you find yourself having to share that country with the grandchildren of people your own grandfathers went around the world killing, only proof of superiority? When you've signed a lifetime contract for a model that's now outdated but there's no get-out clause? When you realise that you've been sold a pup?

Enter a new Robinson who is not, as the latter-day fictional Robinsons have been, publicity-shy: Tommy Robinson (aka Stephen Lennon, Stephen Yaxley, Paul Harris and several other names). Born in Luton in 1982, Robinson remarks in his autobiography that 'I've always been comfortable in a bloke-orientated environment'. (Also: 'I don't "do" romantic much if you hadn't noticed!') He was a member of male gangs at school and then his local football gang:[73] 'My social life pretty much revolved around being out with the lads on Friday nights, then the big day out on Saturday and all that involved – from boozing and chanting all the way to a good old ruck with the opposition.' This is traditional British male behaviour of a kind, and it's not limited to one social class. At Oxford University, the former prime minister David Cameron and his pals (George Osborne, Boris Johnson, et al.) joined a gang not dissimilar to Tommy Robinson's Luton football gang – the Bullingdon Club, which was also loosely linked to sport (in the case of the Bullingdon, hunting and cricket) and which also involved a dress code, much alcohol and formulaic violence.

Cameron became a Tory MP in 2001 and was leader of the party from 2005 to 2016. Tommy Robinson was briefly a member of another gang, the British National Party, and in 2009 co-founded his own gang, the English Defence League, which opposed Islamic extremism but in its rhetoric and demonstrations targeted Muslim people more generally. Both Cameron and Robinson have referred to migrants in derogatory terms (in

2015 Cameron spoke of 'a swarm of people coming across the Mediterranean'). Both Cameron and Robinson have cultivated a 'man of the people' image (there are almost as many press photos of Cameron drinking beer in a pub as there are of Nigel Farage) and both have played the patriotism card – the card that everyone wants in their hand because it trumps not only most others but even, if played cleverly, the patriotism card of your opponent. Cameron was educated at Eton and Oxford; Robinson comes from a different social class and feels disenfranchised but can still play this card: 'I'm just an ordinary bloke who got tired of being a second-class citizen in his own town and his own country.' Repeat: 'I consider myself an ordinary bloke who wants his kids to grow up in a fair, democratic and tolerant country. But I'm also an ordinary bloke who thinks the odds on that happening aren't particularly bright, not the way we're going.' And: 'My over-arching crime, at least in the eyes of the British establishment, has been to be a patriot.'

The patriotism button pressed by both Cameron and Tommy Robinson is adjacent to the one labelled 'British values'. Robinson refers to 'simple patriotism and a respect for our heritage, values and tradition' without any spelling out – and without feeling any need to spell out, as if those things were just givens and automatically good. In a 2014 article for the *Mail on Sunday* to mark the 799th anniversary of Magna Carta, Cameron defined 'British values' as 'a belief in freedom, tolerance of others, accepting personal and social responsibility, respecting and upholding the rule of law' – 'To me they're as British as the Union flag, as football, as fish and chips.' These values are 'vital to people in other countries' too, Cameron concedes, 'but what sets Britain apart are the traditions and history that anchors [*sic*] them and allows them to continue to flourish and develop'.[74] Ah, 'traditions and history' – from which every political party has selectively drawn to bolster their agenda, and mostly from the very long one-bloody-war-after-another strand ('this sceptred isle, / This earth of majesty, this seat of Mars'). The whole 'tradition' of England to which both Robinson and Cameron subscribe is overwhelmingly male and military: castles, commemorations of battles, royal princes getting married in full-dress army uniform. Right-wing nationalist parties routinely use Battle of Britain imagery in their publicity (the BNP and Britain First both managed to choose pictures of Spitfires that in fact were flown by Polish pilots). Tommy Robinson dates the beginning of the English Defence League to the day in March 2009 when a march through Luton by a battalion of the Royal Anglian Regiment, returning from Afghanistan, was protested by Islamic groups: 'We send these lads off to fight in Iraq and Afghanistan and all kinds of worldwide hellholes. If they can't march back through a British town in recognition of their service, then we really have lost the war.'

Tommy Robinson notes that 'for as long as this island has been a nation state, the working class have been very much appreciated when it came to giving them a gun, shoving them in a trench and sending them off to die on the orders of the snooty and superior upper classes', but when 'that same working class sees alien ideologies taking over its communities, when its own families are being racially victimised, and when entire areas are effectively being ethnically cleansed of non-Muslim people, the working class are suddenly the bad guys for standing up and speaking out against it'. This is what Tommy does: stand up and speak out, to and on behalf of an audience that is mostly (I'm guessing but I'm pretty sure) male, white and feeling beleaguered/confused/angry. That's his tribe.[75] Tommy Robinson's gang wars – school, football, anti-Islam – are all tribal. Cameron's Bullingdon Club was tribal, and the whole Tory austerity programme was tribal.

To legitimise and maintain their hierarchy, tribes worship ancestors, looking back more than around or forward. How far back? Three hundred years, say: look through a telescope, back through the smoke of industry and the blood of empire, and you see a white man, no woman in sight, building a wall and training a black man to be his servant.

★

Iain Crichton Smith, *The Notebooks of Robinson Crusoe*: 'How childish to expect justice from a wandering story book.' Childish, perhaps, to expect justice from *anywhere*.

Crusoe: 'I descended a little on the side of that delicious vale, surveying it with a secret kind of pleasure (tho' mixt with my other afflicting thoughts) to think that this was all my own, that I was king and lord of this country indefeasibly, and had a right of possession.'

The poster boy: white man, muscular and ageless,[76] lord of his sunlit island by a sort of divine right – and although, in Walter de la Mare's very fine phrase, 'Islands, like most things, are very largely what they seem', in 'descended', 'delicious vale' and 'secret kind of pleasure' there is surely sexual as well as territorial 'right of possession' being claimed (and advertised by 'afflicting thoughts').

He had a knack for DIY, as long as he didn't have to work to a deadline. Anything else? On his island he was hard-working and God-fearing, as those who pressed the book into the hands of generations of schoolchildren could rightly demonstrate, but he wasn't an especially *good* man. Before the island, he was a slave trader;[77] and when he and a Moorish boy, escaping from their Turkish captors, are rescued by a Portuguese ship, Crusoe sells the boy to the ship's captain. After the island, in *The Farther Adventures of Robinson Crusoe*, despite all that repenting of his wicked ways and his lifetime subscription to God, his attitude to non-white people remained the same: 'I look'd upon these savages as slaves, and people who, had we any work for them to do, we would ha' used as such, or would ha' been glad to have transported them to any other part of the world.' So much for Rousseau's suggestion that isolation is 'the surest means of raising oneself above prejudices'.

He had a great PR team. The contradictions – courage and cruelty, Christian faith and acceptance of slavery, fleeing security and then tedious diligence to acquire security – are what make Crusoe interesting, but for the purposes of those who used Defoe's novel as an educational tool they were edited out.[78] Billed as an emblematic Englishman, Crusoe is barely English ('my father being a foreigner of Bremen'). Billed as a homemaker (and adopted into the 'hard-working families' rhetoric), Crusoe could hardly wait to quit the homes of, first, his parents and then his own family. In *The Farther Adventures*, afflicted by a 'distemper of wandring', he abandons his young children to the care of his widow friend and embarks on a ten-year excursion in which, after revisiting his island, he travels to Madagascar, Southeast Asia, China and Siberia.[79] Friday is killed, and Crusoe 'would have been very glad to have gone back to the island, to take one of the rest from thence for my occasion, but it could not be'. (If he *had* taken another Friday, Walter de la Mare notes, he 'would as likely as not have called him Monday Morning'.) He trades in opium and makes money and is not impressed by the local cultures: the Chinese have built a 'mighty nothing call'd a wall' (Crusoe is an expert on walls) but 'in the main are meer beggars and drudges'; Siberia is a land of 'ignorance and paganism'. Comparing 'the miserable people of these countries with ours, their fabricks, their manner of living, their government, their religion, their wealth and their glory (as some call it)', Crusoe declares, 'I must confess I do not so much as think it is worth naming, or worth my while to write of, or any that shall come after me to read'.

For the British especially, a large part of the appeal of *Crusoe* has been the location (of the central section, usually isolated from the before-and-after sections): the island. The 20-something miles between Dover and Calais may be the most psychologically significant 20 miles in the geography of the planet: 'what sets Britain apart,' David Cameron wrote in the Magna Carta speech quoted above, is its history and traditions, and this *setting apart* is a recurrent trope in speeches by politicians of all parties on the subject of Europe, or speeches that aim to stir patriotism. (In the Magna Carta speech Cameron declared that his favourite book was *Our Island Story*, a history of Britain written for children and first published in 1905.) *We* are different, *we* are special – look, we are separated by clear water from everyone else, so it must be so. Editing Crusoe into poster boy was abetted by Crusoe's island being 'beyond change and chance' – 'utterly remote in its latitude of 9 degrees 22 minutes north of a line even less tangible than any known to a cartographer, utterly uninhabited, enshrining and embosoming in its greenery' (Walter de la Mare). It was fudged: loosely based on the Pacific island Alexander Selkirk was marooned on, 700 kilometres off the coast of Chile, but shifted to the Caribbean and endowed with a climate supportive of both grapes and penguins. The island is 'a region of pure fantasy' – and thus, precisely, nowhere.[80]

For 300 years this country has taken as a role model a man who was a slave trader and who reckoned women as being for no other purpose than 'of service' and people of other colour as 'savages' and took no interest in his children and assumed entitlement. For 300 years this role model has served to embed racism and misogyny in the fabric of British society. The poster wasn't Blu-tacked to the wall of my childhood bedroom; it didn't need to be because Crusoe was there, a ghost, in every room of the house and in the places we walked or drove to.[81]

Imagine being born in England as a female in 1719: your whole existence was to serve men; opportunities for education and professional employment, almost zero; your body at the mercy of male doctors; and if you stepped out of line you could be hung as a witch. To survive, you accepted this as the norm. Imagine, too, being born in 1719 as a man.

Imagine being born in the UK as a woman in 1819, 1919, 2019. Imagine being born in the UK in those years with the colour of your skin not white. Over 300 years, changes have been grudgingly made by those who have had the power to authorise them – slavery abolished, the franchise extended, access to education and employment widened – but in 2019 we are *still* arguing about equal pay for men and women, women's right to control of their own bodies, and racism on the streets and in politics and in the media.

Many books and films have a premise built into their set-ups – for example, that one particular caste has complete dominion over the rest of society – that you just have to swallow, take as a given, while reserving the right to insist that the logic of its playing-out is 'realistic'. Implausibility is frequent in life's set-ups too. As a child, the first day back at my secondary boarding school after the long summer holiday was a shock: entering the gates, I was in a closed world where daily life was governed by an elaborate set of rules that were, most of them, bizarre. Among the things I could get punished for: hands in pockets; staying under a cold shower for fewer than ten seconds, counted (slowly) by a prefect; running when I should be walking, walking when I should be running. Within 24 hours I – all of us – had accepted this closed world as the norm; and *that,* the speed with which we adjusted, was even more depressing than the silliness of the rules.

In 1719 *Robinson Crusoe* brought onto the page certain assumptions of its time – that slavery is OK and can be squared with Christianity, that the function of women in society is to serve men, that people whose skin colour is not white are savages – and *did not challenge them*. The book's long-lasting popularity – not least among those who took it upon themselves to decide what *should* be popular, which books to offer to children (*Crusoe*) and which not (*Moll Flanders*) – largely derives from this failure to challenge: 'For popularity,' writes Walter de la Mare, 'is often little more than the smile that comes into the face of a generation seated before its favourite author with palm outstretched, asking not a bluntly truthful delineation of its fortune or accomplishments, but for a dose of artful flattery. And flattery takes many disguises.' The elevation of *Robinson Crusoe* into the canon of English literature has perpetuated its own assumptions about what is 'normal', which is then argued as the 'natural' way of things.

This isn't exactly news.

Robinson Crusoe has had a 'get out of jail free' card because, not least, it was (arguably) the first English novel and because of the status accorded to literature generally within the culture – a status complicated by the yoking of English literature to empire and to patriotism, whose own pairing is another complication. Simple in design, with strong contrasting colours overriding any psychological shading, *Crusoe* became a *flag* for empire and travelled in the luggage of the merchants, missionaries and generals. The early history of the novel coincided with the expansion of the British Empire; literature became a subject for academic study, with all the apparatus of professorships and certificates, when the empire was at its height. Walter

Raleigh, who was appointed in 1904 to the newly established Chair of English Literature at Oxford University, wrote with pride about these links: 'We have spread ourselves over the surface of the habitable globe, and have established our methods of government in new countries. But the poets are still ahead of us, pointing the way. It was they, and no others, who first conceived the greatness of England's destinies, and delivered the doctrine that was to inspire her.' The team leader is, of course, Shakespeare: 'His works are not the eccentricities of a solitary genius; they are the creed of England . . . He has an enormous tolerance, as well befits the greatest poet of a race which has taught the practice of tolerance to Europe . . . His poetry, which overflows and sometimes confuses his drama, is the highest reach of the only art in which England has attained to supreme excellence.'

More than a century later, Raleigh's sentiments are still in play. The assumption that poetry is the thing the English do better than anything else – although out of 130 UK Nobel Prize-winners, just eleven have won the prize for literature (and five of those were not born in the UK). The assumption, built into the syllabus of the School of English at Oxford over which Raleigh presided, that 'English Literature' comprises a stable corpus of works by white men, plus a few white women – although the composition of that corpus has mostly depended on a group of white men sitting in committee and appointed there by other white men. The assumption that 'our methods of government' are better than any others. The assumption of superiority. Within the academy, these assumptions were challenged in the 1970s and '80s by critical theory, which argued that literary works cannot be independent of the social and political conditions of their making, and that they propagate the ideologies of dominant status groups, but outside the academy they still thrive:[82] literature is still believed to yield 'universal truths' and to be, in some moral if not medicinal way, *good for you*, and English lit is the best on the market, beware of imitations.

When, aged seventeen, I told my uncle that I was going to university to study English literature, he asked: 'And where's *that* going to get you?' Fair question. Another fair question he could have asked but didn't: 'What *is* English literature?' Did – and do – I mean *British* literature? Probably yes, if by British lit what's meant is the literature of the British Isles (including work written not in English), and by English lit what's meant is literature written in the English language by writers across the world, but the whole matter is perennially confused: Margaret Drabble, for instance, in the preface to her edition (2000) of *The Oxford Companion to English Literature*,[83] states that some 'foreign authors' have been included 'in the context of English literature, and I mean English literature, not literature in English, which is another matter entirely', but doesn't spell out what she does mean by 'English literature' because she assumes that I just know.

What I *think* Drabble means is what Walter Raleigh meant: a literature coloured red on the map, with other literatures – Scottish, Welsh, American, 'African', 'Caribbean' – accorded provincial or colonial status. 'Eng Lit' is often a bonus button to be pressed after clicking on 'British values' – whose clumsy spelling out by David Cameron I've quoted above: first the list of platitudes ('belief in freedom, tolerance of others', etc.); then the insistence that these things are as British as the flag, fish and chips, and *football* (just 33 per cent of the players named in the English Premier League squads at the start of the 2018/19 season were eligible to represent England in the national team; just four of the twenty managers were British; just seven of the twenty clubs were British-owned); then the concession that the values of freedom and tolerance are hardly a British monopoly; then empire and entitlement ('what sets Britain apart are the traditions and history') and the implication that *our* freedom and toleration are better than yours.

My own generation – or at least, the tiny bit of it that I spend time with: *my* tribe, one of whose customs is talking to each other about what we've been reading – is the last to look back on a pre-internet childhood and can be a little sentimental about books, taking it as read that books are a Good Thing almost irrespective of their content. I grew up as a reader, and books have been important in my life as, among things, a way of earning an income (books as trade); and this little book about a book is very bookish, and I'm as dismayed as anyone by the continuing closures of libraries and bookshops; but I've never believed literature to be as fundamental a part of the culture as it is assumed to be, or not in such a self-congratulatory way. A *Guardian* report in 2013 on one of those periodic surveys of reading habits was headlined 'Four million UK adults never read books for pleasure' – as if this was *news*. At the time *Robinson Crusoe* was published, the literacy rate for males in England was around 40 per cent, and for females 25 per cent.[84] Educational reforms in the 19th century pushed these rates much, much higher, but from almost the start of the 20th century – not just since the 1950s – literature (Stratford-upon-Avon tourism aside) has been becoming more marginal, less central.[85] Moreover, from the time of *Crusoe*'s publication until very recently, the whole business of books – the writing, the publishing, the critical assessment – has been largely controlled by middle-class white males; and that literature has been awarded a shiny badge and *Robinson Crusoe* has been given a reserved seat has suited that elite. Good morning, Mr Crusoe.

★

It's raining, and Robinson is sitting at an inside table in the café, and because footfall is light the waitress has sat down too and they are playing chess. She has just taken Robinson's last castle with a pawn, and Robinson is feeling restless.

Let him go. Give him a bag of stale bread to feed to the ducks in the park. Give him a bus pass and let him maunder through the suburbs, unrecognised, nostalgic for his parrot. He's old and he's tired and it was never his intention to become a role model, or even to be still around.

The waitress clears the chessboard and the mugs from the table. She sits down next to a fly-specked photograph of the local football team and lights a cigarette. The lino near the door has worn through, there's dust on the poster frames and mice droppings behind the fridge. The whole place is shabby: it needs a make-over, she thinks. Or rather: we need some new narratives. She starts stacking the chairs. She's in charge today, and she's closing early.

The Abyss

In his sermon delivered in the church of St Mary le Bow in London to the Society for the Propagation of the Gospel in Foreign Parts in February 1719 – two months before the publication of *Robinson Crusoe* – Samuel Bradford, Bishop of Carlisle, declared that non-Christian indigenous peoples 'know not their Maker; they are, as it were, without God in the world; they are uninstructed in the only method which God hath appointed of approaching him, by a Mediator; they are insensible of the great Concernments of their immortal Souls, and very much uncertain, at best, in their apprehensions of a future life; they are abandoned to their lusts and passions; and under the dominion of Satan.' He was radicalising his congregation.

Spurred by commercial interests, early British colonialism had the blessing of the Anglican Church. Crusoe instructs Friday – and, later, in *The Farther Adventures*, the other members of his fledgling colony – in Christian doctrine. By the end of the following century the churchmen were out their depth: increased firepower accelerated slaughter, and bogus scientific proofs of the racial superiority of the Caucasian peoples justified the results. 'It seemed obvious,' Sven Lindqvist writes in *'Exterminate All the Brutes'* – the title from a line in Conrad's *Heart of Darkness* (1899) which Lindqvist reads as a four-word summation of the whole colonialist programme – 'that some racial natural law was at work and that the extermination of non-Europeans was simply a stage in the natural development of the world.' Everything conspired towards this conclusion, even Darwin: 'At some future period, not very distant as measured by centuries, the civilised races of man will almost certainly exterminate, and replace, the savage races throughout the world' (*The Descent of Man*, 1871). 'After Darwin,' Lindqvist writes, 'it became accepted to shrug your shoulders at genocide. If you were upset, you were just showing your lack of education.'

Lindqvist's book documents the eradication of indigenous peoples across the world by the European powers. This is recorded history. It happened long ago and in faraway places, but Lindqvist argues that 'Europe's destruction of the "inferior races" of four continents prepared the ground for Hitler's destruction of six million Jews in Europe', which brings it *home*. Colonialism and all it entailed was not a new phenomenon. Peter Levi: 'As the Greeks got richer, and the Romans richer still, the whole world around them was troubled. First they traded, then they adventured, then they colonised and slaughtered and enslaved. That is the whole early history of Europe.' After Europe, the world tour: 'From the sixteenth century on, the British treated every native people in the world they could get at in much the way they had learnt to treat each other. The natives of North America and Australia were massacred in the full light of the nineteenth century. It was a successful method, and it lasted nearly four hundred years.' Then back to Europe: lowest estimate of casualties in the 1914–18 war, 8.5 million; highest estimate, 21 million; and just to think of the difference between those figures is to be faced with the sublime carelessness of the most powerful nations about the expendable lives even of their own citizens. And then. And then. Levi was writing during the Troubles in Northern Ireland: 'Does anyone think that the trouble in Belfast can simply be reasoned away?

Perhaps it can in the end; I believe so, but that is part of believing in the human race. We who do so have a lot of evidence against us.' And now.

Colonialism and empire were successful for *who*?

Not the slaves; nor the people whose centuries-old villages were destroyed in an hour by cannon fired from steamboats, nor the uncounted millions who died from displacement, disease and starvation. Not, also, a large proportion of the citizens of the home nation.

In 'A London Address', written while he was living for a week in 2012 above the Queen Elizabeth Hall in London's Southbank Centre in a suspended boat modelled on that on which Conrad sailed up the Congo in 1890, *Le Roi des Belges*, Sven Lindqvist recalls reading Jack London's *The People of the Abyss* (1903) at the age of nine: 'It was the first *real* book I read. It was real in the sense that it was not a fairy tale for children, or an adventure story made up for boys. The Abyss really existed.' The Abyss was a term used in the early 1900s (notably by H. G. Wells) for the districts in cities in which people lived in extreme poverty.

The American writer Jack London happened to be in London for the coronation in 1902 of Edward VII, an occasion to show off the might of empire: 'here they come, in all the pomp and certitude of power, and still they come, these men of steel, these war lords and world harnessers . . . The rain is pouring down. Up the street come troops of the auxiliaries, black Africans and yellow Asiatics, beturbaned and befezed, and coolies swinging along with machine guns and mountain batteries on their heads, and the bare feet of all, in quick rhythm, going *slish, slish, slish* through the pavement mud.' He wasn't fooled: 'Vivat Rex Eduardus! They crowned a king this day, and there has been great rejoicing and elaborate tomfoolery, and I am perplexed and saddened. I never saw anything to compare with the pageant, except Yankee circuses and Alhambra ballets; nor did I ever see anything so hopeless and so tragic.'

He wasn't fooled because he was living and writing at the time – on the streets, in workhouses, as a lodger – in the East End. Jack London called Trafalgar Square, where he watched the coronation procession, 'the very uttermost heart of the empire', but he was wrong – the uttermost heart of the empire was *here*: ten days after the coronation, walking along Mile End Road, Jack London notices that his two companions repeatedly stoop to the pavement to pick things up, which he assumes are cigar or cigarette butts, but then he looks again: 'From the slimy sidewalk, they were picking up bits of orange peel, apple skins, and grape stems, and they were eating them. The pits of greengage plums they cracked for the kernels inside. They picked up stray crumbs of bread the size of peas, apple cores so black and dirty one would not take them to be apple cores, and these things the two men took into their mouths, and chewed them, and swallowed them; and this, between six and seven o'clock in the evening of August 20, year of our Lord, 1902, in the heart of the greatest, wealthiest, and most powerful empire the world has ever seen.'

Jack London was a journalist as well as a novelist, and had done his research: '1,800,000 people in London live on the poverty line and below it, and 1,000,000 live with one week's wages between them and pauperism. In all England and Wales, eighteen per cent of the whole population are driven to the parish for relief, and in London, according to the statistics of the London County Council, twenty-one per cent of the whole population are driven to the parish for relief. Between being driven to the parish for relief and being an out-and-out pauper there is a great difference, yet London supports 123,000 paupers, quite a city of folk in themselves. One in every four in London dies on public charity [i.e., 'in the workhouse, the infirmary, or the asylum'], while *939 out of every 1000 in the United Kingdom die in poverty* [my italics]; 8,000,000 simply struggle on the ragged edge of starvation, and 20,000,000 more are not comfortable in the simple and clean sense of the word.' Life expectancy in the West End of London, 55 years; in the East End, 30 years. This was a society waging war on itself; war had become the only thing it knew how to do.

Death, in the Abyss, is always knocking on the door. 'Broken by hardship, ill fed, and worse nourished, [the people of the Abyss] are always the first to be struck down by disease, as they are likewise the quickest to die.' 'They feel, themselves, that the forces of society tend to hurl them out of existence. We were sprinkling disinfectant by the mortuary, when the dead waggon drove up and five bodies were packed into it. The conversation turned to the "white potion" and "black jack," and I found they were all agreed that the poor person, man or woman, who in the Infirmary gave too much trouble or was in a bad way, was "polished off." That is to say, the incurables and the obstreperous were given a dose of "black jack" or the "white potion," and sent over the divide. It does not matter in the least whether this be actually so or not. The point is, they have the feeling that it is so, and they have created the language with which to express that feeling – "black jack" "white potion," "polishing off."' 'Then there are the "dangerous trades," in which countless workers are employed. Their hold on life is indeed precarious – far, far more precarious than the hold of the twentieth-century soldier on life. In the linen trade, in the preparation of the flax, wet feet and wet clothes cause an unusual amount of bronchitis, pneumonia, and severe rheumatism; while in the carding and spinning departments the fine dust produces lung disease in the majority of cases, and the woman who starts carding at seventeen or eighteen begins to break up and go to pieces at thirty.' 'With the sweat-shops, married women who eke out their husband's earnings, and single women who have but themselves miserably to support, determine the scale of wages. And this scale of wages, so determined, is so low that the mother and her three children can live only in positive beastliness and semi-starvation, till decay and death end their suffering.' 'In England, every year, 500,000 men, women, and children, engaged in the various industries, are killed and disabled, or are injured to disablement by disease.' 'In the West End eighteen per cent of the children die before five years of age; in the East End fifty-five per cent of the children die before five years of age. And there are streets in London where out of every one hundred children born in a year, fifty die during the next year; and of the fifty that remain, twenty-five die before they are five years old. Slaughter! Herod did not do quite so badly.' 'Poverty, misery, and fear of the workhouse, are the principal causes of suicide among the working classes. "I'll drown myself before I go into the workhouse," said Ellen Hughes Hunt, aged fifty-two. Last Wednesday they held an inquest on her body at Shoreditch. Her husband came from the Islington Workhouse to testify. He had been a cheesemonger, but failure in business and poverty had driven him into the workhouse, whither his wife had refused to accompany him. She was last seen at one in the morning. Three hours later her hat and jacket were found on the towing path by the Regent's Canal, and later her body was fished from the water. *Verdict: Suicide during temporary insanity.* I, for one, from what I know of canals and workhouses, should choose the canal, were I in a similar position. And I make bold to contend that I am no more insane than Ellen Hughes Hunt.'

Jack London entered the East End as a colonialist adventurer: 'I went down into the under-world of London with an attitude of mind which I may best liken to that of an explorer.' And what he found there, as the colonists found in other countries, was a population deemed inferior: 'a new and different race of people, short of stature, and of wretched or beer-sodden appearance . . . a breed strikingly different from their masters' breed, a pavement folk, as it were, lacking stamina and strength'. And for all his deep sympathy with the plight of the people he is living among, and his anger at injustice, many of his responses to the people of the East End chime with the opinions of the most outspoken imperialists of the period: 'These men of the spike, the peg, and the street, are encumbrances. They are of no good or use to any one, nor to themselves. They clutter the earth with their presence, and are better out of the way.'

In 1902 the British Empire was at its height, wealthy beyond compare, and what was happening in the Abyss, in the capital

The East End, London, 1902: photo by Jack London

city of empire, Sven Lindqvist suggests, was a 'quiet, peaceful genocide, accepted and agreed, even by those who would be the next to be killed', perpetrated by those with power over the powerless, within their own country. In *'Exterminate All the Brutes'* Lindqvist notes that of the many millions who died in Latin America following the arrival of European colonisers in the early 16th century, the great majority 'did not die in battle. They died quite peacefully of disease, hunger, and inhuman labor conditions.' Also in the East End of London. Jack London: 'One is forced to conclude that the Abyss is literally a huge killing-machine . . . In London the slaughter of the innocents goes on on a scale more stupendous than any before in the history of the world.' Did he worry that he was being sensationalist? He must have known that his words would be read as such, because in journalism sensationalism is stock-in-trade. I don't think he worried much. At least as shocking to him as the wretched conditions in the Abyss was

Jermyn Street, West End, London, 2019

that they were accepted as normal, even 'natural': 'The people of England have come to look upon starvation and suffering, which they call "distress", as part of the social order. Chronic starvation is looked upon as a matter of course. It is only when acute starvation makes its appearance on a large scale that they think something is unusual.'

Jack London, though aware that the Abyss had been created 'by the artful and spidery manipulation of industry and politics', concluded that the solution was 'a question of business management': 'In short, society must be reorganised, and a capable management put at the head. That the present management is incapable, there can be no discussion.' But the *management* of the Abyss was not the point; it was in exact accord with how the empire was managed: let the weak die, the sooner the better, for the sake of Progress and Civilisation.

The sense of entitlement that propelled the Western colonial and then imperial enterprise, and the dismissal of the powerless as inferior beings, are conspicuous in *Robinson Crusoe*: 'I look'd upon these savages as slaves, and people who, had we any work for them to do, we would ha' used as such, or would ha' been glad to have transported them to any other part of the world; for our business was to get rid of them, and we would all have been satisfy'd, if they had been sent to any country, so that they had never seen their own.' In *The Farther Adventures*, an English seaman who 'had taken a little liberty with a wench' in Madagascar (he raped her) is killed by the local people; in revenge, the English 'kill'd or destroy'd about 150 people, men, women, and children, and left not a house standing in the town'; Crusoe himself thinks they have gone too far, but the boatswain assures him 'that they did nothing but what was just, and what the laws of God allow'd to be done to murtherers'.

That entitlement – which has always been white male entitlement – is still evident in so many of the daily transactions that living in the UK is made up of: in who cleans the streets and the sheets and the toilets; who is served, who serves; in the gender pay gap; in the policies of the Conservative Party relating not just to immigration but to every aspect of social welfare. Those are obvious examples; there are others buried so deep in the default mindset of the past 300 years that most of the time they are invisible. I'm writing this on a day in January 2019 when the overnight temperature is going to be sub-zero and the number of people in London who will be sleeping rough on the streets is several thousand.

Notes & Asides

1 [*Walter de la Mare's* Desert Islands and Robinson Crusoe *(1930)*]
On pages 9 to 58, an essay; from page 59 through to 288 de la Mare
goes vagabonding like Crusoe chasing a runaway goat, riffing
from phrases in the main essay on any subject with a claim to relevance. Those subjects include: Darwin on the *Beagle*; misers; body-
snatching; De Quincey's intake of laudanum ('warm, and without
sugar') and the contrasting effects of cannabis; Byron's funeral; geol-
ogy; space exploration; maps; the spice trade; flat-earthers; islands
that vanish ('the governments of England and Norway were only
recently at odds concerning an island which neither could afterwards
locate'); the price of slaves; Defoe's descendants (a great-grandson
was hanged at Tyburn for highway robbery in 1771: 'one cannot
look upon life for many generations anywhere with complete com-
posure'); trees that 'can move sluggishly from place to place', can talk
to one another and 'are of the usual two sexes'; goats ('it is curious
that no castaway, in spite of ample leisure, ever seems to have tried
to teach a goat to talk'); a dream in which the body of Napoleon is
exhumed, and a childhood memory of staring with horror at a plate
of jelly; parrots and other birds; talking to oneself; quotations from
translations of *Crusoe* into Latin, Dutch and Italian; hermits; death.

2 [*Frederick Brereton*]
Lt.-Colonel Frederick Sadleir Brereton, CBE (1872–1957), author
of the introduction to my 1953 edition of *Robinson Crusoe*, fought
in the Boer War and the First World War and was, according to

Wikipedia, 'an author of children's books on heroic deeds conducted in the name of the British Empire'. His other titles listed in my ancient copy of *Indian and Scout*, which has a bookplate stating it was awarded as a Merit Prize to Fred. W. Kelvey of Dollar Public School in 1922, include *With Shield and Assegai: A Tale of the Zulu War* and *With Rifle and Bayonet: A Tale of the Boer War.* Joyce's *Ulysses*, Eliot's *The Waste Land*, Woolf's *Jacob's Room* and Cicely Hamilton's *Theodore Savage* were all first published in 1922, but it was never likely that the headmaster of Dollar Public School was going to choose any of those to present as a Merit Prize. I suspect that by 'perfectly normal Englishman' Brereton meant simply that he reckoned Crusoe was very much like himself.

3 [*'a prodigious Consumption of our British Manufactures'*]
Defoe's *Weekly Journal* proposal is quoted in Maximillian E. Novak, *Daniel Defoe: Master of Fictions*, OUP, 2001.

4 [*no one was calling it a 'novel' at the time*]
According to the title page of the first edition of Crusoe, it was written 'by Himself'; following rumours of Defoe's involvement, he admitted he may have done some editing of Crusoe's manuscript, then finally came clean: OK, I made it up. If Defoe invented the English realistic novel, he did so by accident, not intention. Observing the birth of the novel is like watching a chicken hatching from an egg; it may not want to be born, but its time has come.

5 [*despatched to Virginia and Maryland*]
In Defoe's *Moll Flanders* (1722), Moll's mother is transported to the American colonies 'for a certain petty theft scarce worth naming, viz. having an opportunity of borrowing three pieces of fine holland of a certain draper in Cheapside'. Moll herself is transported for stealing 'two pieces of brocaded silk'.

6 [*'leaving out all the dull parts'*]
Defoe was incensed by the piracy and abridgements of *Crusoe*. In

the Preface to *The Farther Adventures of Robinson Crusoe*, he calls any abridgement 'as scandalous as it is knavish and ridiculous; seeing, while to shorten the book, that they may seem to reduce the value, they strip it of all those reflections, as well religious as moral, which are not only the greatest beautys of the work, but are calculated for the infinite advantage of the reader'. He challenged those who stole his work to show how their actions differed from highway robbery – and if 'they can't shew any difference in crime, they will find it hard to shew why there should be any difference in the punishment'.

7 [*flaws of the original attracted*]
I can't think of a single other well-known work of fiction that could survive having its opening and closing sections lopped off – which is what many of *Robinson Crusoe*'s rewriters did to it – and still be accepted as a coherent novel. The book would have had a different structure, I think, if the manuscript had arrived on the desk of Charles Monteith – the editor at Faber who, looking at the manuscript of another island novel in 1954, William Golding's *Lord of the Flies*, after it had been rejected by around twenty other publishers, decided that the opening section, which involved a nuclear explosion to get to the start-off, needed to be cut.

8 [*family tree*]
Le Vrai Arbre de Robinson survived the Franco-Prussian War and the Paris Commune and two world wars and was still there in the 1960s, on the rue de Malabry, when I was at school and Ian Nairn was researching the byways of Paris for *Nairn's Paris* (1968): 'I saw it on a misty, melancholy day at the end of October when there was nobody there, the cafés were empty, the lovely chestnut leaves were within a few days of falling and the *tristesse* was intolerable.' But it's gone now. Half a century after Nairn, I went to the site of Le Vrai Arbre on the rue de Malabry myself, and except for a woman whistling for her lost dog there was again nobody there, again an intolerable *tristesse*, but no tree house. In its place, a developer's sign on a boarded-up façade promised luxury flats with timber balconies

overlooking 'une vue époustouflante'. Behind the façade – through a narrow passage with a broken-down gate – was a mess: half demolition site and half rubbish dump, no work going on.

9 [*converting him to Christianity*]
In his 1719 sermon Samuel Bradford argues that masters have nothing to fear from the conversion of 'the poor Negroes from Africa' to Christianity because 'the Power they have over them . . . would not be altered by their becoming Christians, provided they use that power as becomes Christian masters, with the moderation they ought to exercise towards their servants'; rather, conversion would have the 'mighty advantage' of 'making them in the first place, servants to our great Lord and Master in Heaven, and much better servants to their earthly masters at the same time'.

10 ['*who admired Defoe*']
Frank Budgen (in *James Joyce and the Making of Ulysses*, OUP, 1972): 'Joyce was a great admirer of Defoe. He possessed his complete works, and read every line of them. Of only three writers, he said, could he make this claim: Flaubert, Ben Jonson and Ibsen. *Robinson Crusoe* he called the English Ulysses.'

11 [*and J. M Coetzee*]
Marooned in my own language, I'm very dependent upon translators and I haven't read, for example, Saint-John Perse's 'Images à Crusoé' (1909) or Patrick Chamoiseau's *L'Empreinte à Crusoé* (2012) or Julio Cortázar's radio play *Adiós, Robinson* (1984), in which Crusoe and Friday return to an island now boasting more skyscrapers than empty beaches, and on which Crusoe's exploration is restricted to what an official tourist guide permits.

12 [*a traditional English pattern*]
Do I mean 'a traditional *British* pattern'? I probably do. Knowing when to write England and when Britain is an abiding riddle. Orwell in his essay 'England Your England' (1941) admits that 'Welsh and

Scottish readers are likely to have been offended because I have used the word "England" oftener than "Britain", as though the whole population dwelt in London and the Home Counties and neither north nor west possessed a culture of its own'. 'Britain' is largely admin-speak; 'England' carries so much freight as to be suffocating. Even without Crusoe's having become an English/British national myth, I find being English myself – a little Scottish mixed in, maybe a little Irish, but nothing that shows – deeply confusing. (A good part of what I write is about confusion: being told that the world works in one way but experiencing it in different ways.) Orwell's evocation of an Englishness that 'is somehow bound up with solid breakfasts and gloomy Sundays, smoky towns and winding roads, green fields and red pillar-boxes' is the opposite of helpful. This isn't an Englishness that has anything to do with my current life – my breakfasts are not solid, my Sundays not gloomy – and yet I see it *there*, lurking, horrible, in too many books and films and TV shows, not least in the ads in the commercial breaks and in political rhetoric. It teases, grimly: is it something that exists or something that I've been *told* exists, and what's the difference anyway? Orwell follows up his sketch of Englishness with a curse: 'Good or evil, it is yours, you belong to it, and this side the grave you will never get away from the marks that it has given you.'

13 [*they send Karl in for bread, beer and bacon*]
This scene is echoed by that in Jim Jarmusch's 1986 film *Down by Law* in which a Delamarche-and-Robinson duo, played by Tom Waits and John Lurie, on the run from the law with a naive foreigner played by Roberto Benigni, send the latter into a roadside café to check what it has to offer. He finds a sympathetic woman, as does Kafka's Karl. It's a regular male fantasy.

14 [*Brunelda in a film by Fellini*]
In *Intervista* (1987), Fellini films his own attempt to film an adaptation of Kafka's *Amerika* at Cinecittà, the studio in Rome where he had made many previous films. After serial interruptions – by ele-

phants, confetti, auditions of strangers picked up on the metro, commercials, a Japanese TV crew, a joyful reunion between Marcello Mastroianni and Anita Ekberg a quarter-century after they made *La Dolce Vita* – he finally manages to film the scene in which Brunelda takes a bath, aided by Robinson (who, faithful to Kafka, slurps sardines straight from the tin) and Delamarche. Then Brunelda is in a wheelchair, being wheeled through the mud 'to the whorehouse'. A thunderstorm erupts. The cast and crew take shelter for the night beneath a makeshift frame of timber struts and polythene sheets. At dawn they are attacked by Native Americans on horseback wielding not spears but TV aerials. Guns appear in the shelter, the wagon-trail corral, and are fired into the air. Then the director calls cut and everyone goes home through the slush and the cold, wishing one another a happy Christmas.

15 [Robinson in Ruins *(2010)*]
Keiller's *Robinson in Ruins* was filmed during 2008, the year the wheels came off the banking industry. The script of the film, not started until March 2009, acknowledges that background: when the Lehman Brothers employees were running out of their offices with their 'belongings' in cardboard boxes (impossible to carry a cardboard box with any degree of dignity), 'it seemed possible, for a moment, to imagine this was no ordinary crisis, and that some larger, historic shift might be coming'. But by early 2009 that moment had already passed: the wheels were stuck back on, we were going to muddle through, we didn't trust ourselves to do things in any other way.

16 [Jack Robinson *(1933)* by *George Beaton*]
For starters, more play with pen names: Beaton is Gerald Brenan, who had Bloomsbury Group connections and is best known as the author of *The Spanish Labyrinth* (1943) and *South from Granada* (1957). Growing up, he enjoyed neither school nor his home life, and disliked his father – an ex-infantry officer in the Boer War who 'had a mania for giving orders in a sharp, rude voice, for the consciousness of exercising power was his greatest pleasure' – with a vengeance:

111

'He belonged to an utterly different species of humanity from myself.' Aged eighteen, Brenan set off in secret with a friend to walk to China; they got as far as Bosnia, a tramp of more than 1,500 miles.

The second and last book Brenan published under the pen-name George Beaton was *Doctor Partridge's Almanack for 1935* (1934), which purports to be a series of fragmentary prophecies by Dr Partridge, astrologer and author of almanacs, with a preface by 'G. Robinson, Practising Astrologer'. (Dr John Partridge, 1644–1715, was a historical person. In 1708 Jonathan Swift, writing as Isaac Bickerstaff and with the intention of exposing Partridge's quackery, predicted that Partridge would die on 29 March of that year; when Partridge wrote on 2 April that he was still alive, and advertised in newspapers that he was 'not only now alive, but was also alive upon the 29th of March in question', Swift replied that his statement was demonstrably untrue, as 'no man alive ever writ such damned stuff as this'.) According to G. Robinson's introductory account, Partridge died in 1727 and was buried in a cellar under a house in Fitzroy Street; 190 years later, he is stirred back into life by a rat nibbling his finger; learning from nearby talkative bones of the current state of the world ('Is there never to be an end? Must the world grow more bloodthirsty and more feeble-minded with every century?'), Partridge determines to offer 'to mankind a complete calendar and recital of their fate' – 'less with the view, I doubt not, of converting them to the hard creed of Cessation than of relieving them now at this present of some of the fever of life by cutting off their expectancy'.

As outlined in a second preface, this one by 'Professor Blish', the world view of 'our great Partridge' holds that 'discord, folly, strife and confusion [are] the permanent condition of the world and of each separate human being', and humankind must therefore 'learn to look forward with a perpetual increase in longing to the great reconciler and deliverer – that is, to death'. Dr Partridge is a doomy fanatic, but unlike others of that ilk he has a light touch. Some sample entries . . . January 9: 'If you wish to obtain a reputation for stinginess, give a large dance or evening party.' January 31: 'This is a good day for poets and novelists to burn their manuscripts, for painters to tear to

pieces their canvases and for lovers to put their heads into gas-ovens.'
February 1: 'On this day a man called Timothy Pippin will found
a New Religion of universal love, in which all those who do not
believe are to be anathematised, imprisoned, tortured, flayed, and
roasted.' March 22: 'This is an unlucky day for those who collect
tram tickets and while away their lives gazing at rivers and seas.' May
28: 'On this day the world will *not* come to an end, however many
reasons there may be for desiring it.' June 13: 'If you have not lost
anything lately, pray to St Anthony of Padua and he will lose it for
you.' November 11: 'On this day the European nations will give up
their offensive weapons, such as hockey sticks and motor horns and
insect powder, and take to strictly defensive ones, such as tanks and
aeroplanes and poison gas, which are much more likely, as everyone knows, to keep off war.' December 26: 'O world, world, world,
world, if you do not come to an end before next year is out, I, Dr
Partridge, have done with you.'

Brenan later distanced himself from *Jack Robinson* ('there is no
book of mine that I dislike more') but he remained fond of *Doctor
Partridge's Almanack*, for 'a certain command of language as well as
a pessimism that seems to forecast the days of Stalin, Hitler and the
atom bomb'. His explanation of the *Almanack* is almost a recipe:
memories of the First World War and of a doomed love affair, along
with 'some rather inappropriate Old Testament imagery', 'combined
to set up an atmosphere of horror, disgust for life and melancholy
that is so far-fetched that it is always on the point of toppling over
into absurdity'.

17 [*My mother kept many lists, as did Crusoe*]
Here's the list that comprises the first section of Iain Crichton Smith's
The Notebooks of Robinson Crusoe, titled 'Resources': Hogshead of
Bread / Rice / 2 Fowling Pieces / 2 Pistols / 2 Saws / 1 Axe / 1
Hammer / 4 Powder Horns / 5 Bags of Nails / 1 Screw Jack / 12
Hatchets / 1 Grindstone / 3 Iron Crows / 2 Barrels of Musket Bul-
lets / 7 Muskets / 1 Hammock / 1 Roll of Sheet Lead / Bedding /
Small Ropes / Twine / 1 Piece of Canvas / 1 Barrel of Gunpowder

/ 3 Large Runlets of Rum / 1 Box Sugar / 1 Barrel Flour / 2 Cables / 3 Razors / 1 Pr. Scissors / 12 Knives / 1 Large Mirror / 1 Bible / 1 Soul / 1 Body'.

It's not exactly Crusoe's list – Crusoe didn't have saws, and I don't think he had a screw jack either – but it's very Crusoe-esque. 'Is there any book in the language where mere things, goods and chattels, are at once so commonplace and so engrossing?' asks Walter de la Mare. Crusoe is constantly listing his *things* (and also counting his blessings: that he didn't drown with the other sailors in the shipwreck, that he was able to salvage many useful items from the wreck, that his island is fertile and sustains him). He also records measurements, quantities and times in precise detail (it's possible that Crusoe is on the autism spectrum). Making lists is a way of taking of possession, of staying in control; it's a means to survival. My mother, on her own island of widowhood, made many lists; in a small maroon notebook she recorded every Christmas gift she gave between 1956 and 2003, the handwriting becoming almost illegible in the last years, and how much each one of them cost – gifts to family but also to the milkman, the postman, the paper boy, the bin men, the butcher and her hairdresser.

A list of brute facts stuns anxiety into submission. Lists particularise – humanise – the big abstractions: the columns of names on war memorials, for example, like a roll call at school.

Most lists – shopping lists, 'to-do' lists, income and expenses – are non-literary. 'So finding a list in a book or poem,' Francis Spufford notes in his introduction to *The Chatto Book of Cabbages and Kings*, 'is an immediate reminder of the most obvious difference between literature and every other kind of non-performing art: literature is made out of something, language, that is an everyday stuff.' The lists in *Robinson Crusoe* anchor the novel as 'everyday stuff'. Neither Defoe nor Crusoe pretends to elegance or style or imaginative daring. *Crusoe*, Walter de la Mare remarks, 'taxes no ordinary intelligence. There is nothing complicated, delicate, abstruse, subtle to master . . . Its thought is little but an emanation of Crusoe's seven senses and of his five wits.' *Robinson Crusoe* is anti-intellectual: this (and, de la Mare again, Defoe's 'sublime naivety') is what made it so amenable to being abridged to fit an agenda, and to being co-opted into the education system. There's nothing to argue with (lists are not arguments). The novel itself is a kind of *thing*, a tool like a spade or hammer, and was recognised by many as a useful one.

If Crusoe – Defoe, really – *had* been more imaginative, or even more thoughtful, he'd have likely gone under. Imagination comes at a price. Crusoe survives largely because he looks no further than what's in front of him; Frederick Brereton refers approvingly to his 'typically Anglo-Saxon stolidity'.

18 [*continue to appeal*]

George R. Tweed, a US Navy radio operator who hid in the jungle on the Pacific island of Guam rather than surrender to the Japanese in 1941 and survived for two years and seven months, titled his memoir *Robinson Crusoe, USN* (1945). Many Russians who kept diaries during the siege of Leningrad (1941–4), surviving without food or running water, compared themselves to Robinson Crusoe. Polish citizens who went into hiding in Warsaw after the failure of the 1944 uprising became known as the Robinson Crusoes of Warsaw.

An anonymous poster on an internet book forum in September 2018, responding to the question 'How did reading *Robinson Crusoe* as a youngster make you who you are today?', told of bullying and violent sexual abuse during their childhood; they found a copy of *Crusoe* in a box of water-dmaged books that was being thrown out, and the book gave them strength and hope – if Crusoe survived, so could they.

19 [*girls as well as boys*]

Walter de la Mare: 'One cannot escape the misgiving that really "sensible" women at any rate might deal with all this truck about islands much as if it were the rubbish left behind him by a schoolboy gone back to school.' Rose Macaulay challenged him, and he recorded her challenge in a later edition of his book: 'Girls do like islands, you know – as much as boys, I am sure. I mean the normal, average girl . . . It was my own pet game and day-dream always, and I know so many females who always read island stories with delight. I wonder why gentlemen so often make such strange mistakes about ladies? I don't think ladies do it so much about gentlemen – there must be some psychological reason, I suppose. You say, "sensible women". But most women aren't, very; anyway, not throughout. The most sensible might have some island weakness.'

Polly Flint in Jane Gardam's *Crusoe's Daughter* on Crusoe: 'He was like women have to be almost always, on an island. Imprisoned.'

20 [*nor have I have suggested that they do so*]
I didn't *dis*courage them. Children should read what they want to read, including books that are not necessarily 'age-appropriate' and that they cannot fully understand (adults too: not understanding can be one of the pleasures of reading). But the 18th-century language, including words whose meanings have changed since Defoe used them, is a problem, and – for readers more used to contemporary YA novels – the wordiness of the style. I doubt that many people now, children or adults, read *Robinson Crusoe* for pleasure. Robinson *who*?

21 [*without any acknowledgement that women even exist*]
Rousseau fell in love with an illiterate waitress and washerwoman named Thérèse Levasseur who was employed at the hotel in Paris where he lodged. She bore him five children, and each was taken by the midwife to the foundling hospital (in order, Rousseau claimed, to save Thérèse's 'honour': they were not married). Pioneering in his writing on the education of boys, Rousseau was more conservative in his views on women: 'Arrange it so that they love the cares of their sex, have some modesty, and know how to watch over their house-holds and keep themselves busy in their homes.'

22 [*Edward Everett Hale*]
'I was born in the year 1842, in the city of New York, of a good family, though not of that country, my father being a foreigner of Bremen, who settled first in England' – this is the resourceful hero

of Hale's *Crusoe in New York* (1880). He serves an apprenticeship as a carpenter, then builds an elaborate stockade on a vacant lot in New York where he and his mother live for twelve years, growing corn and beans and keeping goats. He rescues a nineteen-year-old Swedish immigrant girl named Frida from 'a crew of devils who knew nothing of love or of mercy' and, surprise, marries her.

Hale's *Boys' Heroes* (1886) includes – in addition to Robinson Crusoe – Hector, Horatius, Alexander the Great, Hannibal, King Arthur, Richard the Lionheart, Bayard, Israel Putnam, General Lafayette, Napoleon and Ralph Allestree: in sum, Crusoe plus ten military commanders plus one invented hero (Allestree, 'an old New England name') who fought on the right side in the 'war of the rebellion' and didn't own slaves and was 'as chivalrous as Richard and as brave as Horatius' and 'never touched liquor'.

Cicely Hamilton in *Marriage as a Trade* (1909) on 'modern chivalry': '[it] has been narrowed down, if not in theory, at least in practice, to a code of deferential behaviour affecting such matters and contingencies as the opening of doors, the lifting of hats, and the handling of teacups; but not touching or affecting the pre-eminence and predominance of man in the more important interests of life. At its best, such a code of behaviour is a meritorious attempt to atone for advantage in essentials by self-abnegation in non-essentials; at its worst, it is simply an expression of condescension.'

23 [*going to a secondary modern*]
https://www.theguardian.com/news/2017/may/04/grammar-schools-secondary-modern-11-plus-theresa-may: 'As the social cachet of grammar school places rose, so the stock of the standard secondary modern and the technical schools declined. They quickly came to be seen not as a valid alternative choice, but as second-, third- or fifth-rate versions of grammar schools. The 11-plus test came to be widely feared and disliked as a crude rationing mechanism that the well-informed could manipulate.'

24 [*reading the Scriptures*]

The guest castaways on *Desert Island Discs*, the BBC radio programme that has been running since 1942, are told that they will be marooned with the Bible and the complete works of Shakespeare and are invited to choose one other book. For their free choice of book, just ten castaways in the programme's online archive (eight men, two women) have chosen *Robinson Crusoe*. In October 2016 a research consultancy asked 2,042 British adults if they'd want to be given a copy of the Bible: 56 per cent said 'No' and another 13 per cent said 'Don't know'.

25 [*public school*]

Another vocabulary riddle: in the UK, public schools are in the private sector. They are called public because they developed out of the schools established centuries ago to offer an education free of Church authority and with access not restricted to families linked to trade guilds. There are only around 1,200 public schools in the UK (and most have charitable status) but their stranglehold on British society has made a truly public and comprehensive system of education impossible to attain.

26 [*my first boarding school (aged eight to thirteen)*]

Gone, now. There was a sex abuse investigation and the school closed in late 2014. It is currently being redeveloped into private housing and a 'psychological trauma care facility'. There are online photos taken by explorers of derelict buildings, and a YouTube video of graffiti being painted on the walls of the swimming pool (opposite) where once, more than half a century ago, I dived in too steeply, hit the bottom and broke off the top of one of my front teeth.

In the online photographs – most taken in 2017 and 2018 – the school buildings resemble the abandoned and looted properties stumbled across by Theodore and Ada in Cicely Hamilton's *Theodore Savage* (1922) as they forage in the post-Ruin landscape. The structure of the original mansion, built in the 1860s for a local businessman by a workforce numbering over a thousand, is intact and, to me, utterly familiar: entering the big front door, I know the patterned red carpet, the elaborate ceiling mouldings and the imposing staircase that leads up to the dormitories. I know that the dining room is on the right and the assembly room is on the left and, beyond that, the headmaster's study and the library, whose windows look onto the cricket pitch. *I know my way around.* Beyond the hallway will be the new-build classrooms; the toilets will be on the right (a central block for peeing; no doors on the cubicles along the walls); a left turn, more classrooms and above them the dormitories for the juniors; at the end, the gym, also used for screening films and the annual Gilbert and Sullivan productions. These more modern parts of the school have declined faster than the original building: invasion of greenery, rusted lockers, peeling walls, wires dangling from collapsed ceilings.

This is Ruin Porn: time, death, loss, waste, the vanity of human ambition embalmed within an aesthetic of decay. The appeal of photographs of buildings abandoned within living memory, or within recent generations, is especially sharp: mortality is catching up fast, is about to overtake. I wanted there to be photographs of the library with *Punch* and the *Illustrated London News* in their binders and a copy of *Robinson Crusoe*, swollen with damp, lying on the floor, and I also didn't want this: the allure of Ruin Porn is too obvious, too cloying.

When I think of *Robinson Crusoe* I think not of a sunlit desert island but of a long, cold corridor in a boys' school in which I am not allowed to run.

27 [*they told me where I was*]
Rules mapped the world, but a part of us always knew that they were not the thing itself. The river was out of bounds; it was spanned by a very old stone arch. Aged thirteen, Michael and I, joint head boys, threw rocks at that arch until the keystone went and it all crashed down, then stood beside the headmaster in assembly while he denounced vandals from the local village.

28 [*the grey building at the top of the village back home*]
This large building was known as the orphanage; it was where the toys my brother and I had grown out of were taken in cardboard boxes, though I never, ever, saw any children there. To get to the orphanage we drove out of the village on a narrow road past the cricket green and the social club where old people played bridge and then turned right onto a faster road. If we turned left towards Horsforth we got into a maze of other small roads and at each further junction I, in the grey Austin A35 or the Ford Anglia with its cheese-slice rear window, was impressed by my mother's knowing which way to turn. What was stopping us getting lost? Knowledge of which way to turn arrived, I assumed, with adulthood; I just had to trust, and wait.

29 [*war and animals, mostly*]
Before Forester and Haggard and Buchan and all the other books I read at the age of around twelve, there was *Exploration Fawcett* (1953), compiled from the letters and diaries of Colonel Percy Fawcett (1867–1925?) by his youngest son. Fawcett was in the Crusoe mould, a gritty survivor in alien lands. In search of the lost city of Z, rumoured centre of a pre-Columbian civilisation in the Brazilian state of Mato Grosso, Fawcett set off on his last expedition in 1925. At the end of May he sent a message that he, his eldest son and one other companion were

about to enter territory never previously explored by Europeans; and then they vanished. Later expeditions sent to discover what happened to Fawcett returned only with rumours and the wrong bones. Among the theories: that Fawcett and his companions were killed because they had run out of gifts to placate the indigenous people; that Fawcett became chief of a tribe of cannibals; that his secret real intention had been to found a commune based on the theosophical notions of Madame Blavatsky.

About the whole story there's a Crusoe-esque, batty Englishness, and this includes my reading the book as a solitary child in my comfortable bedroom in a dormitory suburb of Leeds.

If there was something legendary about Fawcett – and there was and still is: the film *The Lost City of Z*, based on his last expedition, was released in 2017 – I think it's because he did the right thing. I think explorers are *supposed* to disappear. After you've discovered the source of the Nile or the Northwest Passage or the lost city of X, what next? Sit at home watching TV?

30 [*school holidays*]
The school holidays: other than some very long bike rides, I remember little of what happened during this downtime. What *didn't* happen (and should have happened: this is every teenager's right) was visiting the untidy bedrooms of friends and spending hours lazing around listening to weird music, because being at boarding school for most of the year – the first school around 40 miles from home, the second school around 200 miles – I didn't know anyone I could visit. Crusoe missed out on this too, and it's an important stage.

31 [*a different life*]
Did my mother have delicious self-pity nights like my own at school? I never asked. Certain topics were not discussed; that language is inadequate we took for granted. Sex, religion, politics: a holy trinity, an English and very Crusoe tradition (he did do religion, but in a wholly conventional way: like the weather, really). No one sat me down – does it have to be done *sitting down*? – and explained things.

There was a time when I didn't know certain things and then a time when I did, or at least I had an inkling. I think now, though I haven't always, that this wasn't far worse than talk. Explanations only get you so far, and most leave you as floundering as before. I suppose it depends on who is doing the explaining.

I did once begin asking a question that seemed to be about contraception and I was sent to the family doctor and he was more embarrassed than I was. When I opted out of religion – I refused to go through the ritual of confirmation – no one batted an eyelid. I'd been expecting opposition, some attempt to persuade me out of my opting out, but no one took it seriously enough, or personally enough, to make that attempt; and that *I* was taking it seriously was cause for embarrassment so best ignored. About politics, I think my mother *was* serious. Living in a solidly Tory constituency, with no hope of a Labour candidate being elected to parliament, my non-Tory mother joined the local Conservative Party in order to have at least a say in who was going to be their candidate, a canny move, but I don't remember that we talked about this – not even during the washing up (my mother washing, me drying, my brother putting away) or in the car, when we didn't have to look at one another.

On summer bank holiday Mondays the whole family – uncles, aunts, cousins – would assemble in Roundhay Park for a picnic, and when it rained we sat defiantly in our cars in the car park with our egg sandwiches.

32 [*wartime rationing*]

Rationing is Crusoe: the small supply of rum he rescues from the ship he makes last for a quarter of a century. Here's a Crusoe-like little list of the rations – per person per week – of certain foodstuffs at the end of the Second World War in the UK: bacon, 4 oz; tea, 2 oz; sugar, 8 oz; cheese, 2 oz; meat, 1s. 2d. in value; eggs, rare. Other items that were rationed: soap, petrol, clothes, paper.

Rationing and thrift are now a kind of folk memory, but there's an affinity between wartime rationing and the austerity policies of the Tory government which the UK voted into power in 2015. A streak of masochism here, a Crusoe-esque (and public-school) belief that hardship and suffering are good for you. The same streak was operating in the vote on the EU in 2016. Certainly in play in that referendum – in which most of the old voted to quit, most of the young to remain – was a simplified, sentimentalised version of wartime Britain: the Blitz, coming together in adversity, Britain standing alone against the might of Germany. Set against that story-book picture, the EU, portrayed in the media for years before the referendum as meddling and super-bureaucratic, didn't stand a chance. Britain was never a fully signed-up member in terms of commitment; we were always arguing for opt-outs and pay-backs. The EU is complicated; complexity arouses suspicion; the *Crusoe* model of one man on his island is as simple as it gets.

33 [*unearned entitlement upon which the empire had subsisted*]
Sweetwater Memories (1984), a TV documentary, included interviews with British national service troops who had served along the Sweet Water Canal in Egypt in the early 1950s. One, a dog-handler, recalled that if his dog had attacked an Egyptian he got treated to drinks in the mess. One remembered being with other soldiers in a truck that picked up an Egyptian girl by the side of the road, a girl in her early teens, and they gang-raped her. They spoke as straightforwardly to camera as if they'd been asked what they'd had for breakfast: no explanations, no apologies, no regrets.

34 [*marching around in battledress with rifles was compulsory*]
The CCF – the Combined Cadet Force – still exists in 400 secondary schools in the UK. 'Each CCF is an educational partnership between the school and the Ministry of Defence,' explains the website, which also states that the government has committed to increasing the number of cadet forces in schools to 500 by 2020.

35 [*except for God*]
At home, a decorative shield hung on the wall of the dining room – not the original, which was made for the Paris Exhibition of 1867,

but a silver-plated copy. The panels of this shield depicted scenes from Milton's *Paradise Lost* and it hung a little awkwardly; it needed a bigger wall. At the top is the Lord God Almighty. Below him, in the central panel, the Archangel Raphael is having a few words with Adam and Eve in the garden, and below that the Archangel Michael is pirouetting over the defeated Satan. On the left side all the good people are ascending to heaven, and on the right all the bad people are tumbling down to hell. To encourage me to eat up my greens, my mother would recount these scenes to me at mealtimes. I don't know why I didn't just eat up, I knew the story and it wasn't even a good one, but this was the ritual. I have a memory of the shield lying flat on a blanket on the table while my mother is polishing it, pressing down hard with the oily cloth into all the crevices where tarnish has settled.

36 [*thrashed your arse with a cane*]
I remember failing to explain to others that Lindsay Anderson's film *If* (1968) was not a caricature. I remember reading somewhere in Auden, around the same time, that the purpose of education was to induce just so much stress as the individual can bear without actually breaking. Aged seventeen, I was anorexic. I dropped out of the rugby team. ('Dropping out' is just a thing you do, barely realising you are doing it; it's not any form of considered opposition. Besides, as a form of licensed violence, I *liked* rugby.) I wrote a play about a boy who ran away from school and on the day of its one performance the boy who was to play the runaway boy ran away, as I did too, more than once, though not very far, just a few miles. I joined the RSPB.

37 [*'a man's body is given him to be trained and brought into subjection'*]
And a woman's body? Thomas Hughes didn't have much to say about this. I think he assumed, like Crusoe, that women's bodies were 'for service': to bear children, clean the house and make supper. The quotation is from Hughes's *True Manliness* (1880).

38 ['*doing the right thing*']
Sacrifice is one of the tick-boxes, high up the list, in the Muscular Christianity curriculum. The classic act of sacrifice by an explorer – explorers were up there with warriors as role models – was that of Captain Oates on Scott's last expedition to the South Pole: suffering from frostbite and gangrene, he walked into a blizzard to die and thereby give his companions, whose progress to safety he was slowing, a better chance of survival. Oates was a brave and selfless man, but except in such extreme circumstances it's surely more important to live for others than to die for them.

39 ['*part of His Glory*']
It was Smith's duty to be Crusoe, not self-doubting. October 1919: 'There has gained in power a new philosophy. The exponents claim that all history, all morality, have been wrongly taught. They regard religion as a device to make the poor humble instead of assertive. This creed has received wonderful impetus from the experiment of politics in Russia, which has succeeded beyond all expectation. This creed maintains that there is injustice in the world as long as the man who does not work with his hands has more wealth or opportunity than he who does; that the wealth of the rich is derived entirely from the work of the poor, and that every poor man has a right to this wealth, which he should acquire by force if possible . . . But this creed recognises nothing spiritual. Its aim is the gaining of money, or what money will buy . . . At this solemn hour there is a menace to religion, to the spiritual and selfless life, a menace that, if it prevails, will bring us to bondage – not of Germany – of Antichrist amongst us.'

40 [*the number was down to 29 per cent*]
Figures from the Sutton Trust (https://www.suttontrust.com/research-paper/parliamentary-privilege-the-mps-2017-education-background/). Percentage of the UK population attending private schools, 7; percentage of senior judges who attended private schools, 71; of senior armed forces officers, 62 (Social Mobility and Child Poverty Commission, 2014).

41 [*an even greater cataclysm*]

The 1914–18 war did not encourage optimism about the future of civilisation. In *The People of the Ruins* (1920) by Edward Shanks, Jeremy Tuft, a university lecturer who has served in the artillery during the war, is told by a lunch companion: 'Don't you know there's a moment in anything – a holiday, or a party, or a love affair, whatever you like – when you feel that you've reached the climax, and that there's nothing more to come. I feel that now. Oh! It's been a good time, and we seemed to be getting freer and freer and richer and richer. But now we've got as far as we can and everything changes . . . Change here for the Dark Ages!' Tuft, who 'held the comfortable belief that mankind was advancing in conveniences and the amenities of life by regular and inevitable degrees', replies: 'Oh! We shall go jogging on just as usual.' Half an hour later a scientific experiment goes wrong; Tuft loses consciousness and wakes in the late 21st century to an England that, after 'The Troubles', has been bombed back almost to the Middle Ages: no telephones, no planes, a few trains (until they all break down), no electricity (except, bizarrely, in a few villages in the Cotswolds, so David Cameron is OK). Tuft joins the London tribe and helps them reinvent guns; the Northern tribe is defeated and Tuft marries the London chief's daughter, but then the Welsh tribe conquer and it all goes predictably wrong. Tuft has a vision in which 'cities would be burnt, bridges broken down, tall towers destroyed and all the wealth and learning of humanity would shiver to a few shards and a little dust'; he kills himself. Historically, what's shocking here is not so much that Civilisation and Progress collapse so fast but that it took the mass slaughter of the 1914–18 war for people to realise their fragility.

E. M. Forster, writing in his *Commonplace Book* in 1943, during the next world war: 'I can't rid myself of the theory that men will stop making & using machines, and revert with a tired sigh to the woods.'

42 [*a simple chap stuck on an island*]

Other versions are available. In Michel Tournier's *Friday, or The Other Island* Crusoe is still centre stage but, as the title indicates, it's

Friday and the island who have the upper hand. Crusoe is introduced as 'pious, parsimonious and pure', and is warned by the captain of the ship on which he is sailing, just before the shipwreck: 'Beware of purity. It is the corrosive of the soul.' During an initial period of despair Tournier's Crusoe experiences a 'breaking of some spring within himself'; no longer able to stand upright – a posture which is only possible in society, where 'the crowd packed around him continues to prop him up' – he crawls on hands and feet, gnaws 'unmentionable foods' and rolls in his own excrement. He regulates his life on the island in traditional Crusoe fashion, finding that 'to build, to organise and to make and abide by rules were sovereign remedies against the demoralising effects of solitude', but in contrast to the always purposeful work of Defoe's Crusoe the work of Tournier's Crusoe is often purpose*less*, and thus a form of play, though involving no less sweat: he spends years carving out terraces with walls of stone for planting corn which he does not in fact possess.

In a moment of self-liberation after his water-clock stops reckoning time, he begins 'to discern *another island* behind the one where he had so long dwelt in solitude, a place more living, warmer and more fraternal, that had been concealed from him by the prosaicness of his daily occupations'. Mandrakes spring up in the place where Crusoe and the island come together in sex, and 'a new man seemed to be coming to life within him, wholly alien to the practical administrator'. Friday arrives. At first docile, Friday resists management, not least by his 'irrepressible, lyrical and blasphemous' laughter and, to Crusoe, his crazy exuberance: he uproots shrubs and replants them 'with their topmost branches in the earth and their roots in the air', the world turned upside down, and the plants still thrive. A gunpowder explosion destroys Crusoe's stockade, and he knows that 'in his heart he had longed for something of this kind to happen'. He learns to live as Friday lives. When a British ship arrives by chance, Crusoe chooses to let it leave without him.

J. M. Coetzee's *Foe* displaces Crusoe even further from Defoe's, setting him apart from a triangular relationship involving the writer Foe, the castaway Susan Barton and Friday. In the first part of the

GOOD MORNING, MR CRUSOE

novel Susan Barton describes being marooned by mutineers on a desert island, her life on the island with Crusoe and Friday, and the death of Crusoe on board a ship taking them back to England. In the second part Susan Barton has become as if the guardian of Friday in England; she addresses Mr Foe, a writer she has engaged to bring her adventures to book; Foe goes into hiding to escape his creditors and the bailiffs. The third part comprises chiefly an exchange between Susan Barton and Foe: her resistance to his shaping of her story, his insistence that the island 'is not a story in itself' and can be brought to life only 'by setting it within a larger story', her belief that 'The true story will not be heard till by art we have found a means of giving voice to Friday' – Friday whose tongue has been cut out, either by the slavers who transported him from Africa or by Crusoe himself, and who ends this section at Foe's desk 'writing the letter *o*' (which could equally be the figure zero). The short concluding part, with no named narrator, 'is not a place of words . . . This is a place where bodies are their own signs. It is the home of Friday.'

The above summary is laughably reductive. Coetzee's novel touches on privilege and power, gender, race, story-telling, colonialism and resistance and freedom; it touches open nerves. (Touch – and the holding back from touch: an etiquette prevails on the island inhabited only by Friday, Crusoe and Susan Barton, all sleeping close – is important; touch, 'soft and cold', is in the last sentence.) In his Nobel Prize lecture in 2003, titled 'He and His Man', Coetzee returned to Crusoe, fiddling with the roles even further: *He* is Crusoe, *His Man* is Defoe, 'that dapper little man' writing reports of decoy ducks ('duckoys') in Lincolnshire, a guillotine in Halifax, the plague in London. Master and slave, brothers, enemies? Deckhands, He thinks, on ships that 'pass each other by'.

43 [*Crusoe has infantilised his readers and followers*]
Even Luis Buñuel's film of *The Adventures of Robinson Crusoe* (1954) offers only two brief glimpses of a Crusoe who is sexually aware. Crusoe erects a scarecrow in his field of wheat and drapes over it a woman's dress, then gazes at the dress wistfully before turning away.

Friday finds another woman's dress in one of the chests rescued from the shipwreck and delights in wearing it, and Crusoe immediately tells him to take it off.

Of course it's very possible that Defoe decided – like the headmaster of an old-school all-boys' boarding school – that because the cast of his novel didn't include women, on Crusoe's island sex simply *didn't exist*. A parenthetical note by E. M. Forster: '[by the way why is D. only keen on the sexual life of women? His approach to men's – in Col. Jack – is quite perfunctory. Only when there is a woman in the case does he warm up]'. This goes back to Genesis (and beyond): Adam was getting along fine until Eve arrived, and then there was the incident involving the snake and the apple, and everything that happened afterwards was all *her* fault. This was a pretty standard male point of view, and still is – but for Defoe, 'a great imaginative writer' (*The Oxford Companion to English Literature*, ed. Margaret Drabble)?

It's an example of a regular problem that readers have with many *great imaginative writers* (Eliot, Yeats, Céline and Philip Larkin for starters) – that they can be both hugely intelligent and gifted and at the same time, about race or sex, bigots – and it has nothing to do with political correctness. It has to do with white male privilege. It has to do with the cards being shuffled at a table in a coffee house in London in early 18th-century London and being dealt a hand of politics, religion, economics and literature, and managing that deal into a winning hand. Literature does not trump the other cards, but used in combination with others it adds points. *Robinson Crusoe* (Defoe was pro-colonies, anti-Catholic, a prominent player in the politics of his time) is a prime example of literature being played to win.

44 [*Robinson is a 'factory manager'*]
Victoria Glendinning, in her biography of Elizabeth Bowen, states that 'the starting point' for Robinson was a man named Jim Gates, 'the manager of a creamery in Kildorrey': 'completely non-intellectual, genial, a life-and-souller'. With Jim Gates, Glendinning writes, Bowen 'had, simply, a good time, with lots of drinks and lots of cigarettes and easy laughter . . . His company was a liberation not

only from the excessive sensibility of others but from her own – that sensibility which was at the centre of her talent and also, some have thought, its limitation'. Bowen, Glendinning writes, 'needed men like Jim Gates: extrovert, practical, a little coarse'. I'm uncomfortable with biographers telling me what their subjects needed or didn't need, but I think I know a Robinson when he turns up.

45 [*narrator of the novel is a film editor*]
Film references are frequently employed as shorthand descriptions of Robinson: he's 'like Orson Welles as Harry Lime in *The Third Man*; that same moon face'; he brings to mind 'Richard Burton in *Who's Afraid of Virginia Woolf?* – a hammy drunken actor trying to play an un-hammy drunk'; or he's 'like a gangster in a Jean-Pierre Melville film'. Watching Robinson, 'trying to gauge him', the narrator notes that 'His gaze became unreadable, as neutral as that of a camera.'

46 [*These and other clichés filled my head*]
James Kennaway's high-octane *Some Gorgeous Accident* (1967) is an earlier example of a novel featuring two close-knit male characters adrift in London on a tide of alcohol and sex. First line: 'Link's love, his speech, his actions, why even his thoughts had overtones of violence; of pain experienced and pain inflicted purposely.' Link is a hard-bitten news photographer: 'There was always a girl; a hilarious disaster; jokes and pokes. Where are you at, Link, now?' Fiddes – who is loved by Link 'like a brother; a younger, sadder, if no more serious brother' – is a doctor who (like Céline's Bardamu) is dedicated to working with the poor but who is far from idealistic (working for no money: 'There was such awful, English arrogance in that'). They are 'Two egos. Well matched; ill met.' In a Mayfair bar Link despises the 'smooth-chinned cardboard men with no city for a soul, men prefabricated with mini-motives harmlessly inbuilt, men incapable of good or evil, with matching golf-clubs in their this-year cars'; off the Harrow Road he knows 'You're no different, Link, to all the other miserable hunted punters and kerb-crawlers hereabouts, just a man on your own with a bald-headed dog in your pants; that

habit-forming dog. Do this, do that, wee girl . . .' In the out-patients waiting room at St Stephen's Mission Maternity Home – a 'tiny, triangular room' – Susie, Link's girl, falls in love with Fiddes. A meddling nurse accuses Fiddes of performing an illegal abortion on a prostitute; Link does not actively discourage her, and the case goes to trial. Fiddes is struck off the medical register. Susie runs from them both; she is knocked by a lorry into a snowdrift, picks herself up ('A tragic figure of fun, just right for the film directors who are all so anxious to say something about futility and the cold and all that') and flies off to Rome, leaving Link and Fiddes with their vodka and beer.

47 [*writing about status, power and money*]
Writing about sex is not easy, and nor is writing about writing about sex. 'Defoe sandwiches sex between the laundry bills and the faith of a mercantilist in a just and affluent society' – I copied that down from a 1965 article in the *Guardian* about Defoe because I like the sound of it but I'm not at all sure what it means.

48 [*not unhappy with his deal*]
At the end of Defoe's novel, which allots about half a sentence to Crusoe's marriage, several pages are given over to the arrangements by which Crusoe recovers his profits from his plantation in Brazil for the years in which he has been absent, arrangements spelled out in excruciating financial detail ('Secondly, there was the account of four years more . . . and the balance of this, the value of the plantation encreasing, amounted to 38,892 cruisadoes, which made 3,241 moidores . . .'). Crusoe concludes his story by, in effect, signing off a set of company accounts: he sells his plantation and his agent 'sent me bills of exchange for 32,000 pieces of eight, for the estate; reserving the payment of 100 moidores a year to him, the old man, during his life, and 50 moidores afterwards to his son for life, which I had promised them, which the plantation was to make good as a rent-charge. And thus I have given the first part of a life of fortune and adventure, a life of Providence's chequer-work . . .'

49 [*Crusoe has a dream*]

After he becomes aware that he is not always alone on his island, Crusoe has other dreams: 'I dream'd often of killing the savages, and of the reasons why I might justify the doing of it.' He also dreams that one of the prisoners of the cannibals escapes and comes running towards him – and this is exactly what happens: a prisoner is rescued by Crusoe, who then makes him a servant. The uncanniness here is not in the dream itself but in the literal accuracy of its foretelling.

In the forty-one poems and prose poems that comprise Iain Crichton Smith's *The Notebooks of Robinson Crusoe* (1975), Crusoe's dreams and memories – 'O that I were a man without memory, a machine renewed by the days' – are more troubled and confused: they include sex, violence, Western movies and childhood comics. 'Today I wished to write a story,' section 6 begins, and the story is a reversal of the eventual liberation of Defoe's Crusoe from his island, throwing wide open the whole notion of rescue: '[a story] of a man wrecked on an island for many years, feeding on fish and flesh, limes and oranges, who rushing down a long slope to meet his rescuer (in punctilious blue) would run through him bone and sinew to the other side'.

50 [*more general afterthoughts*]

Walter de la Mare on the *Serious Reflections*: after the opening essay on solitude, 'They afterwards ramble off into a sermon on honesty and similar themes – prolix, sententious, laboured, with a digression that in passing scornfully dismisses the arts and courtesies of the Chinese, even their porcelain – "if we had the same Clay we should soon outdo them". As for their silks, gold and silver, "they have nothing but what is not common with our ordinary poor Weavers". A sublime insularity.'

51 [*above the power or reach of the allurement*]

Forgive me for existing, says the waitress in the café where Robinson is a regular customer. Forgive me for being such a hindrance to your righteousness. It's obviously my fault you have to go to such strenuous efforts to ignore me. We're closing early. (No, says the man who owns the café and has noticed since she has started working here, more customers are coming in. We're not closing. There are two guys over there who are waiting to order.)

52 ['*the mole upon his chin*']
Described at a time when he was 'wanted' for seditious libel for a £50 reward: 'a man middle-sized and spare . . . of a brown complexion, and dark-brown-coloured hair, but wears a wig; a hooked nose, a sharp chin, grey eyes, and a large mole near his mouth'. Virginia Woolf: 'He had a wife and six children; was spare in figure, with a hooked nose, a sharp chin, grey eyes, and a large mole near his mouth.' Jane Gardam: 'He had a lot of disguises – very queer. All those warts, and the stoop.' Ford Madox Ford: 'He may have died a mere Grub Street hack but he shall be a hard, angular pebble indeed for oblivion to swallow.'

53 ['*and then went home and said my prayers*']
Defoe's *Moll Flanders* offers an expanded version of this taking-a-woman-into-the-coach scenario. Moll is picked up by 'a gentleman extremely well dressed and very rich'; he 'asked me if I durst trust myself in a coach with him; he told me was a man of honour'; they go in his coach to Knightsbridge, they walk, he drinks, they go to a house where is known and he fucks her; more drinking; they get back in the coach and he 'was for acting over again what he had been doing before'; Moll resists, he falls asleep, and when the coach has to stop in a narrow street to let another pass by she exits with his 'gold watch, with a silk purse of gold, his fine full-bottom periwig and silver-fringed gloves, his sword and fine snuff-box'.

So far, so obvious; but Defoe presses further. Moll thinks about this 'comely handsome person' who has behaved as men do when they're drunk, 'picking up a common woman, without regard to what she is or who she is', but who doubtless has 'an honest, virtuous wife and innocent children, that were anxious for his safety'. She confides in her fence, the woman who sells her stolen goods. This woman identifies the man and visits him. He is very afraid that he has caught syphilis off Moll, and will infect his wife; the woman assures him that Moll is a 'gentlewoman' and has not slept with a man since the death of her husband eight years before. He insists that he attaches no blame to Moll and admits that if his watch and purse hadn't been stolen by her then the coach driver would probably have pocketed them: 'It was my own folly and madness that brought me into it all; ay, and brought her into it too.' A trading relationship is established (Moll: 'my business was his money, and what I could make of him'): for a period of 'about a year' the man visits Moll, sleeps with her, and pays her sufficiently that she doesn't need to go out stealing on the streets.

54 [*other examples of literary male duos include*]
Male duos in film and TV are also, of course, common: Batman and Robin, the Lone Ranger and Tonto, Butch Cassidy and the Sundance Kid, Starsky and Hutch, and the characters played by Richard E. Grant and Paul McGann in *Withnail and I* (written and directed by Bruce Robinson). If I added in the roll call of British male TV comedy duos (which developed out of the music-hall tradition: there's nothing *new* here), even just those current when I was growing up – Morecambe and Wise, Tony Hancock and Sid James, the Two Ronnies, Peter Cook and Dudley Moore, Harry H. Corbett and Wilfrid Brambell, Alfie Bass and Bill Fraser in *Bootsie and Snudge* among them – the list would run off the page.

55 [*James Kennaway's Link and Dr Fiddes*]
See note 46. Kennaway is actually more interested in threes than twos – triangles allow room for sexual jealousy – but the woman between Link and Fiddes in *Some Gorgeous Accident* is largely a fantasy figure (and the wife of Fiddes stays off-stage, reading poetry).

56 [*authors of all these books are male*]
In *A Room of One's Own* Virginia Woolf teases her audience – 'Do not start. Do not blush' – with a sentence from a (fictitious) contem-

porary novel: 'Chloe liked Olivia.' She then struggles 'to remember any case in the course of my reading where two women are represented as friends'. Of course from the Greek tragedies onwards there have been powerful female characters, but 'almost without exception they are shown in their relation to men. It was strange to think that all the great women of fiction were, until Jane Austen's day, not only seen by the other sex, but seen only in relation to the other sex. And how small a part of women's life is that; and how little can a man know even of that when he observes it through the black or rosy spectacles which sex puts upon his nose.'

57 [*Lars Iyer's* Spurious *(2011)*]
'Here we are at the end of Literature and Culture, stripped, bereft, embarrassed. We are children tromping in old boots.' Thus Lars Iyer in 'Nude in Your Hot Tub, Facing the Abyss (A Literary Manifesto after the End of Literature and Manifestos)'. A belief that one is living at the *end* of something is not unique to now; many people believed this in, say, the 990s and the 1890s; maybe all people over a certain age. The beginning of the particular end that Iyer is talking about is dated back to the decade during which I was at boarding school, moving on from Rider Haggard and Conan Doyle to Lowry and Updike: 'Sometime in the 1960s the great river of Culture, the Literary Tradition, the Canon of Lofty works began to braid and break into a myriad distributaries, turning sluggish on the plains of the cultural delta.' By now, 'Literature' as it used to be known – 'revolutionary and tragic, prophetic and solitary, posthumous, incompatible, radical and paradoxical' – is 'a corpse, and cold at that'; and authors have been replaced 'by a legion of keystroke labourers, shoulder to shoulder with the admen and app developers'. Conclusion: 'Don't be generous and don't be kind. Ridicule yourself and what you do. Savage art, like the cannibal you are.' This is heady stuff, up there with the manifestos of yesteryear.

58 [*'The Philosophy of Umbrellas'*]
Whether or not an umbrella is philosophical, it is a comic piece of

machinery *in itself*: the way it gets turned inside out by a sudden gust of wind; the way the struts get tangled and bent; the way an umbrella confuses any entrance through a doorway and then, once inside, deposits the rain it was designed to ward off; the way an umbrella cannot be employed on a busy pavement without poking out the eye of an innocent passer-by, and cannot be shared by two people without both of them getting wet; the way an umbrella gets *lost* so easily. Stevenson's essay, not least when he asserts some major principle – 'A mendacious umbrella is a sign of great moral degradation' – is couched in this awareness. A sign of the umbrella's respectability is that the quality ones can be possessed only by people who can afford to 'expose twenty-six shillings' worth of property to so many chances of loss and theft'; writing in 1882, in the context of arguments about who should be allowed the right to vote and the fear of those who had got it all sewn up that they might be vulnerable, he suggests ownership of a 'really well-conditioned' umbrella as a deciding condition, 'as worthy of the Franchise'. He reports the observations of 'a scientific friend': 'There is no fact in meteorology better established – indeed, it is almost the only one on which meteorologists are agreed – than that the carriage of an umbrella produces desiccation of the air; while if it be left at home, aqueous vapour is largely produced, and is soon deposited in the form of rain.' The theory to support this phenomenon will, the scientific friend believes, belong to 'the same class of natural laws' which will also explain why a falling slice of toast always lands with its buttered side down.

In early 18th-century England, the umbrella was nicknamed a 'Robinson'.

59 [*campaign medals*]

Walter de la Mare quotes a description by H. M. Tomlinson of an Indian prince sitting in a railway station in Sri Lanka in the uniform and helmet of an English soldier: 'On his breast were displayed a number of ornate decorations, brass regimental badges, and medals won by other people in the past for diverse things – for swimming at Plymouth and running at Stamford Bridge. And central on his breast, hanging by a cord, was a conspicuous red reflector from the rear lamp of a bicycle.'

60 [*a more unnatural, artificial environment*]
Absconding from a society whose silly rules one cannot accept doesn't *necessarily* mean de-humanising oneself. In Italo Calvino's *The Baron in the Trees* (1957), twelve-year-old Cosimo Piovasco di Rondò, ordered to eat snails for lunch one morning in June 1767, runs into the garden, climbs a tree and says he will never come down. He doesn't. 'Like Crusoe,' says the girl he fell in love with as a child and who returns after many years, seeing him dressed in a fur cap and goatskin breeches and how he has improvised his own manner of shelter and hunting and cooking. Unlike Crusoe, he plays a full part in the society from which he has absconded: he is 'a solitary who did not avoid people'. He runs (not quite the right word) errands, helps with the harvest and the vintage, fights pirates, organises a militia to combat forest fires, reads widely and educates others, writes and prints pamphlets, corresponds with Voltaire and Diderot, is visited by Napoleon and has many love affairs. 'You can't have everything,' children are routinely and tediously told. The Baron does have everything: a life lived entirely on his own terms but without isolation from his fellow men and women.

61 [*women were largely excluded*]
Walter de la Mare quotes from *Niels Klim's Journey under the Ground* by the Danish writer Ludvig Holberg, first published in Latin in 1741. Through an opening in a mountain, Klim enters an underworld whose social arrangements prompt many sharp observations on the customs of the European countries that Holberg knew: 'The *English* prefer their liberty to everything else; and none are in this nation slaves, with the exception of the married women.'

62 [*Jane Gardam's* Crusoe's Daughter]
Crusoe post-island: 'I marry'd, and that not either to my disadvan-

tage or dissatisfaction, and had three children, two sons and one daughter' – and nothing more is heard of them until, in *The Farther Adventures*, he gives them into the care of his widow friend (and accountant) and sets off again on his wanderings.

63 [*Elizabeth Bishop's 'Crusoe in England'*]
Few people remember Crusoe after he was taken off the island. (The fight with the wolves in the Pyrenees? The dance with the bear?) Until he recovered the money owing to him from his plantation in Brazil, he had cash problems: 'that little money I had, would not do much for me, as to settling in the world'. He was very, very alone: 'as perfect a stranger to all the world, as if I had never been known there'. Coetzee thinks about this time, as does Elizabeth Bishop in 'Crusoe in England'. Crusoe has been asked by the local museum to bequeath to it his possessions: 'the flute, the knife, the shrivelled shoes, / my shedding goatskin trousers / (moths have got in the fur)'. He is puzzled: 'How can anyone want such things?' He's more isolated and bored in England than he was on the island that was his own to command, and the knife on the shelf that once 'reeked of meaning' now 'won't look at me at all. / The living soul has dribbled away.' He rehearses memories of his life as a castaway: feeling sorry for himself ('What's wrong about self-pity, anyway?'); drinking home brew made from berry juice, then whooping and dancing among the goats; painting a baby goat red with the same berries, just to see some colour; Friday, of course ('he had a pretty body'). 'And then one day they came and took us off.'

One of the poem's lines – 'Home-made, home-made! But aren't we all?' – is echoed in the berating by the narrator in Keiller's *London* of English culture, a harangue so desperate and true that he takes a serious joy in his despair: 'so exotic, so *home-made*'.

64 [*if Crusoe himself had been a woman*]
Walter de la Mare quotes from an account by Isaac James in *Providence Displayed* (1800) of a woman discovered by an English expedition on the shores of a lake west of Hudson Bay in the north of

Canada in January 1772. After her mother, father, husband and child had been killed by men from another tribe and she had been taken prisoner, she escaped and survived for seven months through the winter by building a hut, making a fire from sparks produced by 'by long friction and hard knocking' of two stones, and fashioning snow-shoes, clothes, a fishing net of willow-bark fibres and snares to catch partridges, rabbits and squirrels. She was found 'in good health and condition'. The local men employed by the English expedition fought one another to decide 'who should have her as a wife'. (De la Mare does not mention this part of the account; instead, he rather dreamily associates the woman who 'had spent in solitude the dark icy months of winter' with – 'though it is a long, far call' – Emily Brontë.) One of the seven wives of the expedition's guide objected, 'telling him that he already had more wives than he could properly attend'; he beat her, 'and bruised her to such a degree, that after lingering some time she died'. The names of neither the wife who died nor the woman who survived are recorded.

65 [*Crusoe reinforces his stockade*]
For Christmas 1957 my main present – from my mother – was a model castle. It comprised grey plastic pieces moulded to look like stone, and I slotted them together and placed the fort on top of the upturned lower half of the box it came in, a bit wobbly but printed to look like rock, and played with it for many hours. It had a portcullis and a drawbridge, to keep people out. It cost £1 19s. 11d. We went on holiday to Wales and visited castles and I bought a book about castles. This was a boy thing.

Back then, people in the UK generally called the rest of Europe 'the Continent', much as Crusoe referred to the place where the cannibals came from as 'the main land'.

Rudyard Kipling in *Something of Myself* (1937): 'When my Father sent me a *Robinson Crusoe* with steel engravings I set up in business alone as a trader with savages (the wreck parts of the tale never much interested me), in a mildewy basement room where I stood my solitary confinements. My apparatus was a coconut shell strung on a red cord, a tin trunk, and a piece of packing-case which kept off any other world. Thus fenced about, everything inside the fence was quite real, but mixed with the smell of damp cupboards. If the bit of board fell, I had to begin the magic all over again. I have learned since from children who play much alone that this rule of "beginning again in a pretend game" is not uncommon. The magic, you see, lies in the ring or fence that you take refuge in.'

66 [*all the non-white people in* Robinson Crusoe *as cannibals*]
Outside *Crusoe*, not all 'savages' were cannibals (a label that suited colonialist propaganda). The concept of the Noble Savage was gaining currency, as in Aphra Behn's *Oroonoko* (1688), in which the sublime nobility of Oroonoko and Imoinda is set in stark contrast to the brutality of the white colonisers and the English captain who sells Oroonoko into slavery. Oroonoko leads his fellow slaves in a rebellion: 'We are bought and sold like Apes or Monkeys, to be the sport of Women, Fools and Cowards; and the Support of Rogues and Runagades, that have abandoned their own Countries for Rapine, Murders, Theft and Villainies.' Persuaded by a false promise of pardon, Oroonoko surrenders, and is whipped and tortured. To prevent the pregnant Imoinda from seeing 'this Barbarity towards her Lord', the colonists lock her up – 'which was not done in kindness to her, but for fear she would die with the sight, and then they should lose a young Slave, and perhaps the Mother'.

67 [*the two names don't even sound alike*]
Names. Defoe's father, James Foe, was a tallow chandler; his mother, Annie, died when he was young; the son was ambitious and added the De when he was in his thirties. Defoe also wrote under more than a hundred pen-names (these included Abigail, Anglipolski of Lithuania, Betty Blueskin, Combustion, Obadiah Blue Hat, Sir Fopling Tittle-Tattle, Wallnutshire and Enigma). Kreutznaer into Crusoe is a joke, but a serious one. Ford Madox Hueffer became Ford Madox Ford in 1919 because it wasn't a good time to have a German-sounding name. Some Robinsons were born Rubinstein

or Rabinowitz. At the school Defore attended in Stoke Newington there was a boy named Timothy Cruso; he became a preacher.

68 [*a photograph by August Sander*]
Given that Sander's itinerants are of no fixed abode, their clothes are remarkably clean. W. H. Davies, in *The Autobiography of a Super-Tramp* (1908), defines several categories of tramp, and it's possible that Sander's pair are of the type that 'wanders from workhouse to workhouse; and this man, having every night to conform to the laws of cleanliness, is no less clean, and often cleaner, than a number of people whose houses contain bathrooms which they seldom use'. Another type of clean tramp is the one who 'is proud of being a good beggar, who scorns the workhouse, but who knows well that a clean appearance is essential to his success'. Davies adds that 'the dirtiest looking tramp is often the most honest and respectable, for he has not the courage to beg either food or clothes, nor will he enter the doors of a workhouse'; Sander has photographs of these too.

That Sander's itinerants are allowed, in this photograph, to be 'gentlemen of the road' – dignity intact, independence personified – is a complicating element in the always fraught, voyeuristic relationship between the viewer of this kind of photograph and the subject, and that between the photographer too and the subject. The Polish writer Andrzej Stasiuk describes driving past a Gypsy caravan in Romania, then reversing, 'while Piotr grabbed his Leica and slung his Nikon over his shoulder'. A price is negotiated ('They didn't want money, they wanted cigarettes'). Photographs are taken, then Stasiuk and Piotr drive off. 'We had reduced their humanity to an exotic image, they limited ours to the economy of their own survival.'

Josef Koudelka also photographed Gypsies, and others in the margins. To do so, he turned himself into a vagrant, slinging a sleeping bag over his shoulder along with his camera. A series of self-portraits (2017) show him settling in for the night or waking in fields and streets, and also interiors: Koudelka bedding down on the floor of a bedroom and not the bed, because it's not his; and on the floor of what looks like a living room, in front of an elaborate doll's house.

69 [*increasingly administered*]

Evading administration, staying out of the allotted categories, doesn't come without inconvenience and requires constant vigilance: one small slip and there'll be tax demands and advertising brochures piling up on the doormat. More easy is to get conscripted into this gang or that and end up with a mortgage or a criminal record. The pressure is on, and it shows. Sometimes I want to put my arm round Robinson's shoulders, sometimes I want to wring his neck.

70 [*Weldon Kees's Robinson*]

'The dog stops barking when Robinson has gone': the first line of the first of four Robinson poems by the American poet Weldon Kees – 'Robinson', 'Aspects of Robinson', 'Robinson at Home', 'Relating to Robinson' – written between 1944 and 1949. The line points to the silence that becomes conspicuous, *loud*, when a background noise you've become so used to that you barely register it – a refrigerator's hum, the slur of traffic on a motorway – is suddenly cut off. The poems are echo chambers that resonate with Robinson's absence, an absence all the more insistent for his never having been particularly present even when he was around. 'All day the phone rings. It could be Robinson / Calling. It never rings when he is here.' Glimpses, stills from a film whose plot, if it ever had one, has been forgotten: Robinson playing cards at the Algonquin; at Longchamps, 'staring at the wall'; buying a newspaper; in bed with someone else's wife, drunk and afraid; on a beach in flower-patterned trunks; in East Side bars. Robinson asleep, shape-shifting in dreams: 'A heretic in catacombs, a famed roué, / A beggar on the streets, the confidant of Popes'. Robinson seen in the street one day in early summer, gazing into a shop window, then turning to face the narrator 'with dilated, terrifying eyes' – though the narrator cannot be certain 'that it was Robinson / Or someone else', because Robinson 'Leaves town in June and comes back after Labor Day' and so can be assumed to be out of town.

Kees himself is best known for his own vanishing: on 19 July 1955 his car was found on the north side of the Golden Gate Bridge in

San Francisco, the key still in the ignition, and – barring a couple of unconfirmed later sightings, in New Orleans and Mexico – he was never seen again. His savings account was untouched; in his apartment, the police found a pair of red socks in a sink.

71 [*'the first metropolis to disappear'*]
William Leith's *British Teeth* (2001) is a deceptively slight look at its going – and the going of England – spun around 'a cold February lunchtime, the light drizzle punctuated with sporadic sunshine, [when] I was trying, and failing, to eat a sandwich in the capital city of a country with a serious identity crisis'. The sandwich: a ciabatta, 'an obscure homage to the Mediterranean, to olive oil and fatty cheese, to the sun, to a level of authenticity which was, we must have felt, somehow missing from our lives'. The literature: all those prize-winning novels set in the past. The films: gritty underclass social realism or rom-coms with 'bumbling fools who can hardly speak in coherent English, or do anything much, until a sensible American puts them straight'. The housing: Leith and his girlfriend are looking to buy and they are looking for 'somewhere old', because they want somewhere with 'character', and all the places they are taken to see are badly heated and are held together by cowboy repairs. Draughts, damp, leaks in the roof: these are what character in British housing *is*.

On a train, Leith listens to a conversation between an American woman and a British man from Leeds: she speaks knowledgeably and in detail about her home town and then asks the man what his own home town is like, and he says, 'Dunno, really.'

The British, Leith suggests, have forgotten how to tell their stories; or disagree about what those stories are; or find that the stories they are telling don't tally with the place they are living in; and the result, as he looks around him, is that 'Buildings and streets, whole towns and cities even, seemed insubstantial. They seemed to have been leached of meaning.' Nearly two decades of continuing neglect after Leith finally got his tooth abscess seen to have served only to deepen the housing mess, the divide between rich and poor, and the country's identity crisis.

72 ['*world economy in which we live*']
https://www.telegraph.co.uk/finance/2874177/High-labour-cost-drives-Samsung-out-of-Britain.html

73 [*his local football gang*]
Tommy Robinson's football gang wars were aggressive demonstrations of a kind of white male group identity that *Robinson Crusoe* was used to foster: 'Nothing, not even football,' wrote Thomas Godolphin Rooper in 1903 (see page 31), 'will do more to maintain and extend the dominion of the Anglo-Saxon than the spirit of Defoe's *Robinson Crusoe.*' At the kinds of schools Rooper attended and wrote about, team sports and *Crusoe* both served to instil the hardiness and discipline required for imperial purposes.

During the 1960s, when I was attending Leeds United home matches during the school holidays, Leeds's regular team included Albert Johanneson, one the first black players in top-flight English football and the first to play in an FA Cup final. Every time Johanneson stepped onto the pitch he received racial abuse. After he retired from football in 1971 he had health and alcohol problems; he died alone in a Leeds council flat in 1995, his body not discovered until a week later.

74 ['*to continue to flourish and develop*']
'In recent years,' Cameron adds, tolerance of those who are intolerant has allowed 'extremism – of both the violent and non-violent kind – to flourish'. He believes a more 'muscular' approach is needed. (The last time that adjective appeared here it was attached to 'Christianity'.) To counteract extremism, he is pleased to say that 'proper narrative history' is being brought back into the school curriculum, so that children can learn 'our island's story'. .

75 [*his tribe*]
It's the same tribe that follows Jordan Peterson, another man doing the standing-up-and-speaking-out thing. Peterson gets more airtime and publishing offers because he is an academic and quotes

philosophers. Peterson believes that there are 'natural' (biological) reasons for hierarchies in which men hold power and women don't and that men, faced by challenges to the authority of traditionally masculine roles, simply need to 'toughen up'.

76 [*muscular and ageless*]
Walter de la Mare: 'Crusoe never seems to grow a day older. We are told he was in his twenty-eighth year when he landed on the island, and nearly sixty when he left it . . . But what are mere dates in these matters? For my part he was just the more juvenile side of forty, say, thirty-eight, when he swam ashore from the wreck, and just the more juvenile side of forty he will ever remain.'

77 [*he was a slave trader*]
Crusoe is not Daniel Defoe, but nowhere in the novel is there even an uneasiness about the institution of slavery. Defoe in the *Review*, 22 May 1712: 'The Negroes are indeed Slaves, and our good People use them like Slaves, or rather like Dogs, *but that by the way*: he that keeps them in Subjection, whips, and corrects them, in order to make them grind and labour, does *Right*, for out of their Labour he gains his Wealth: but he that in his Passion and Cruelty, maims, lames, and kills them, is a *Fool*, for they are his Estate, his Stock, his Wealth, and his Prosperity.'

Defoe was a contrary man. His acceptance of slavery as necessary for profitable business is one thing; his belief that Britain is a nation of immigrants and his advocacy for women's education are another. For me, his untiring involvement in public life – what Walter de la Mare calls 'his zest for the attentions of the busy fractious world of men' – is appealing; he made mistakes, he declared bankruptcy (a vast amount owing, he could never catch up), he was imprisoned for debt and put in the pillory for libel, and after each setback – like Moll Flanders, whose own resilience he celebrated – he brushed himself off and started again. My quarrel is less with Defoe than with *Crusoe* and the uses that book has been put to.

78 [*they were edited out*]

Just as, for example, Winston Churchill's racist and imperialist beliefs are edited out of the abiding image of a square-jawed man in his sixties with a cigar clamped in his mouth and his right hand signalling V for victory, plus a few rousing speeches and a very grim statue in Parliament Square. Churchill was present at the Battle of Omdurman in 1898, when 11,000 Sudanese were killed for the loss of just 48 British soldiers and the wounded Sudanese – as many as 16,000 – were executed: this was, Churchill wrote in *The River War* (1899; quoted by Sven Lindqvist), 'the most signal triumph ever gained by the arms of science over barbarians'.

79 [*Madagascar, Southeast Asia, China and Siberia*]

No one who has been marooned on an island for 28 years would find it easy to settle back into society. (For the narrator of Muriel Spark's *Robinson*, the 'man-shaped island' of Robinson comes to resemble, after her return to England, 'a locality of childhood, both danger-ous and lyrical'; and if, while walking in the street or drinking her morning coffee, she happens to remember the island, 'immediately all things are possible'.) For me, the most affecting pages in the whole Crusoe saga are those at the start of *The Farther Adventures*. Back in England, Crusoe cannot let the island go: 'I dream'd of it all night, and my imagination run upon it all day; it was uppermost in all my thoughts, and my fancy work'd so steadily and strongly upon it, that I talk'd of it in my sleep.' His wife is not deaf or blind, and tells Crusoe she knows that if she were dead, he'd be up and away. Crusoe asks if she'd be happy for him to go now. '"No," says she very affectionately, "I am far from willing: but if you are resolv'd to go," says she, "and rather than I will be the only hindrance, I will go with you; for tho' I think it a most preposterous thing for one of your years and in your condition, yet if it must be," said she, again weeping, "I won't leave you; for if it be of Heaven, you must do it; there is no resisting it."' This is the first time in Defoe's writing about Crusoe that a woman is given a voice; it has had to wait until after the basic *Robinson Crusoe* is over, and it's a startling paragraph. She loves her husband; and Crusoe, it turns out, loves her back. They have one child and she is pregnant with a second. (Meticulous in his recording of the number of his barrels on the island, and of his trading profits, Crusoe sometimes loses track of the number of his children.)

Crusoe argues himself out of his 'chronical distemper' and – no need for a therapist – resolves 'to divert my self with other things'. After the sale of his slave-worked plantation, he has no money worries ('and that I had was visibly encreasing'). He buys a farm 'in the county of Bedford': 'I went down to my farm, settled my family, bought me ploughs, harrows, a cart, wagon, horses, cows, sheep; and setting seriously to work, became in one half year a meer country gentleman; my thoughts were entirely taken up in managing my servants, cultivating the ground, enclosing, planting, &c.'

Then his wife (we never learn her name) dies, and 'the world look'd aukwardly round me'. Again, he is marooned: 'She was, in a few words, the stay of all my affairs, the center of all my enterprizes, the engine that by her prudence reduc'd me to that happy compass I was in, from the most ruinous project that fluttered in my head.' Despite the best-remembered quality of his wife being 'prudence', despite her death being a plot device to allow Crusoe to wander off and kill more savages, there's still something happening here that's of more interest than the number of days on the island that it took to make a shelf on which to parade three copies of the Bible. Crusoe rents out his farm to a tenant and returns to London, where 'I had no relish to the place, no employment in it, nothing to do but to saunter about like an idle person, of whom it may be said, he is perfectly useless in God's creation; and it is not one farthing matter to the rest of his kind whether he be dead or alive.' Almost certainly he is clinically depressed. Then a nephew turns up, a nephew who has been engaged by 'some merchants' to go 'on a voyage for them to the East Indies and China' and who suggests uncle Robinson come along, which he does.

So Crusoe runs away to sea again. His first running was from the prospect of a life of comfort and ease which his father had been in position to establish for him ('in easy circumstances sliding gently thro' the world, and sensibly tasting the sweets of living without the bitter'); his second running, after the Bedfordshire interlude – that brief period when he 'enjoy'd the middle state of life that my father so earnestly recommended to me, and liv'd a kind of heavenly life' – is from the same. (For a man of such wealth, status and sobriety, finding another wife after the death of his first would not have been hard.) This is the most interesting thing about Crusoe: that in situations of complete security in normal society, he rebels or gets depressed and is prone to self-destruct; while alone on the island he is diligent and dutiful, and all his effort is towards self-preservation.

80 [*and thus, precisely, nowhere*]
The appeal of 'nowhere' – also known as Utopia – is perennial. (As is the appeal of small uninhabited islands – the kind which, as Walter de la Mare puts it, 'appear on our atlas to be specks as minute as the vagrant footprints of some tiny insect that has strayed into the cartographer's ink' – but this is to dismiss the insects, birds and crabs that do inhabit these islands; and without a means of escape, these places are prisons; and often, they are used as testing sites for military hardware or as detention centres for unwanted refugees.) Amid the dusty clutter of my life I do sometimes hanker after the clean white shell of a new-build apartment (with balcony and a functioning toilet) in which to start over, from scratch – which is what Crusoe did, though not by choice. But then what? An 1874 print by Currier and Ives titled *Robinson Crusoe and His Pets* (opposite) depicts Crusoe in his well-appointed cabin: a cat, a dog, two parrots and two goats gaze meekly towards him; three turtles claw their way onshore, happy to be made into soup; a family of sort-of penguins stand by a canoe looking lost; ropes, a spade and a basket are casually displayed; a musket and axe are propped against a barrel, and a pistol and cutlass hang inside the cabin. The shipwreck is in the background; the whole picture would make a good jigsaw. Crusoe is sitting in a cane chair at his table in smart boots, his gruel and liquor in front of him; one leg is crossed over the other, one hand rests on his knee, his opposite elbow is propped on the arm of his chair; he

Above (Currier and Ives, 1874): Crusoe on the island, living the well-furnished life of ease he had fled England to escape from. Below (1903): Crusoe back in England, writing his *Serious Reflections.*

has no one to talk to and nothing to read except three copies of the Bible, it's nice to have some spares, and he is a Victorian gentleman wondering why the club waiter is taking so long to bring his brandy-and-soda and why his wife wasn't at home when he last checked and he is living in a garden centre in Surrey and he is cashing in on his celebrity by posing for an ad for a company that makes high-class axes and muskets and he is looking very, very bored.

What did David Cameron plan to *do* in the double-glazed, sheep's-wool-insulated, Farrow-and-Ball-painted 'shepherd's hut' that he installed in the back garden of his Cotswolds home in 2017 after he had sunk this country into a renewed pit of racism and walked out the door into 'a portfolio career of charitable positions, business roles and lucrative speaking engagements' (*Guardian*, 17 January 2019)? Back gardens – a subplot in the Englishman's-house-is-his-castle story: it's possible that what the Englishman has always wanted even more than the house, which is a signifier of family, has been a place to get out of the house into, without having to enter public space, and *Crusoe* fed both main and subplot. He was going to write a book, Cameron said, in his cabin with *wheels*, decorative ones, not intended to roll anywhere far.

The frontispiece to volume 3 (the *Serious Reflections*) of a 1903 edition of *Robinson Crusoe* (previous page) depicts Crusoe back in England with a glass of sherry and a decanter on his table but still a cutlass hanging behind him and Crusoe in almost the same position as in the Currier and Ives: again one leg crossed over the other, again one elbow on the arm of his chair, although now the hand that before was on his knee holds a quill: he is writing a book – a book in which he will sermonise that 'life in general is, or ought to be, but one universal act of solitude' – and he is still looking bored.

81 [*the places we walked or drove to*]
In the house where we sometimes went for supper in the 1950s and '60s, a 1930s house in a suburb of Leeds with a garden at the back and beyond the garden a sports field where boys played football and cricket, melon was often the first course, served on a plate with ad-

jacent knife and fork, which cued my uncle's party trick: he would pick up his slice of melon with his hands and munch straight into it and say, with a wink, 'nigger fashion'.

Later, in the 1980s, my wife was asked at a party by a smiling man in a suit: 'And what do *you* do – make babies?' I think he too reckoned he was being witty. He spoke with the kind of bland reasonableness that is characteristic of many of those born into privilege. It says: I'm intelligent enough to know I'm speaking like an idiot and I know that you are intelligent to know that I know, but that's how the system works and you don't seriously expect *me* to change it, do you?

In 2016, during the US presidential campaign, the *Washington Post* published a video in which Trump was recorded saying to a TV host: 'You know I'm automatically attracted to beautiful – I just start kissing them. It's like a magnet. Just kiss. I don't even wait. And when you're a star, they let you do it. You can do anything. Grab 'em by the pussy. You can do anything.' Then media storm. Then a statement on Trump's campaign website: 'This was locker room banter, a private conversation that took place many years ago. Bill Clinton has said far worse to me on the golf course – not even close. I apologize if anyone was offended.' Next, the election of Trump as president of the US.

'Locker room banter'. Golf! Good morning, Mr Crusoe.

82 [*outside the academy they still thrive*]
Inside the academy too. In 2017 students at Cambridge University wrote an open letter to the English Department asking for changes to the syllabus; the *Daily Telegraph* carried a front-page article headlined 'Student forces Cambridge to drop white authors', and then printed an inside-page acknowledgement that they'd got it wrong. Writing about this in the *Times Literary Supplement* (https://www. the-tls.co.uk/articles/public/cambridge-english-curriculum-decolonization), Sarah Jilani noted that 'the sense of inevitability that prevails even among faculty – that they must spend the overwhelming majority of their time on certain (white, male) names out of convention and expectation – tells of the weight of institutionalized norms'.

83 [The Oxford Companion to English Literature]
The entry for *Robinson Crusoe* in Drabble's edition of this OUP reference book summarises only the central section of the novel and makes no mention of Crusoe's slave-trading; the account of Crusoe's life on the island is praised as 'extraordinarily convincing', revealing 'Defoe's gift for vivid fiction'.

(From 1891 to 2010 the *Oxford English Dictionary* gave the second meaning of 'Enlightenment' as designating 'the spirit and aims of the French philosophers of the 18th c., or of others whom it is intended to associate with them in the implied charge of shallow and pretentious intellectualism, unreasonable contempt for tradition and authority, etc.'. According to the Ian Hamilton edition of the *Oxford Companion to Twentieth-Century Poetry*, I was a member of a 'loose association' of poets in the 1950s in New Zealand. Don't believe everything you read in the newspapers.)

84 [*for females 25 per cent*]
Numbers from: https://www1.umassd.edu/ir/resources/laboreducation/literacy.pdf.

85 [*more marginal, less central*]
D. J. Taylor: 'Powered by Victorian educational reforms, the move towards mass literacy and the emergence of a new range of mass-market newspapers and periodicals, reading – once one leaves aside its chief rival, organised sport – had by the early years of the twentieth century become the principle British leisure activity. At the same time, this cultural dominance was extraordinarily short-lived. The mass take-up of radio and cinema was already in prospect . . . [T]he history of English literary culture in the period after 1918 is a history of dissolution . . . Henceforward the world of books, for all its centrality to the idea of "culture" and for all the abstract glamour with which it was attended, would be a minority pursuit, whose decision-making processes, protocols and subject matter would be largely controlled by a cultivated elite.'

References

Anderson, Sherwood, *Winesburg, Ohio* (1919; Penguin, 1992)

Beaton, George, *Jack Robinson: A Picaresque Novel* (Chatto & Windus, 1933)

— *Doctor Partridge's Almanack for 1935* (Chatto & Windus, 1934)

Beckett, Samuel, *Mercier and Camier* (1970; Faber, 2010)

Behn, Aphra, *Oroonoko* (1688; W. W. Norton, 1997)

Bishop, Elizabeth, *Geography III* (Chatto & Windus, 1977)

Bowen, Elizabeth, *Look at All Those Roses* (1941; Cape, 1967)

Bradford, Samuel, *A Sermon Preached before the Incorporated Society for the Propagation of the Gospel in Foreign Parts, 19 February 1719* ('Printed for John Wyat', 1720)

Byrd, William, *The London Diary, 1717–1721: and other writings* (ed. Louis B. Wright and Marion Tinling, OUP, 1958)

Calvino, Italo, *The Baron in the Trees* (trans. Archibald Colquhoun, Harcourt Brace, 1959)

Cameron, David, https://www.gov.uk/government/news/british-values-article-by-david-cameron

Céline, Louis-Ferdinand, *Journey to the End of the Night* (1932; trans. Ralph Manheim, Oneworld Classics, 2010)

Coetzee, J. M., *Foe* (Penguin, 1987)

Cooper, Sam, 'Distant Relatives: Robinson, from Defoe to Keiller' (2011; www.drsamcooper.com/surrealist-research/distant-relatives-robinson-from-defoe-to-keiller)

Davies, W. H., *The Autobiography of a Super-Tramp* (1908; OUP, 1980)

Defoe, Daniel, *Robinson Crusoe and The Farther Adventures* (1719; Collins, 1953)

— *Moll Flanders* (1722; Vintage, 2010)

— *Roxana* (1724; World's Classics, 1981)

de la Mare, Walter, *Desert Islands and Robinson Crusoe* (Faber, 1930; 3rd edn, 1947).

Flaubert, Gustave, *Bouvard and Pécuchet* (1881; trans. Mark Polizzotti, Dalkey Archive, 2005)

Forster, E. M., *Commonplace Book* (ed. Philip Gardner, Scolar Press, 1985)

Franzen, Jonathan, 'Farther Away', *The New Yorker*, 18 April 2011

Gardam, Jane, *Crusoe's Daughter* (Abacus, 1986)

Glendinning, Victoria, *Elizabeth Bowen* (1977; Phoenix, 1993)

Greene, Graham, *The Human Factor* (1978; Vintage, 2005)

Hamilton, Cicely, *Marriage as a Trade* (1909; The Women's Press, 1981)

— *Theodore Savage* (1922; HiLo Books, 2013)

Iyer, Lars, *Spurious* (Melville House, 2011)

Joyce, James, 'Verismo ed idealismo nella letterature inglese: Daniele De Foe & William Blake', lecture, Trieste, 1912, in *Occasional, Critical and Political Writings* (ed. Kevin Barry, OUP, 2000)

Kafka, Franz, *Amerika* (1927; trans. Michael Hofmann, Penguin, 2007)

Keiller, Patrick, *London* (1994) and *Robinson in Space* (1997), BFIVD926

— *Robinson in Ruins* (2010), BFIB1098

— *The Possibility of Life's Survival on the Planet* (Tate Publishing, 2012)

Kennaway, James, *Some Gorgeous Accident* (1967; Mainstream, 1981)

Kipling, Rudyard, *Something of Myself* (1937; Penguin, 1977)

Leith, William, *British Teeth* (Short Books, 2001)

Levi, Peter, *The Flutes of Autumn* (Arena, 1985)

Lindqvist, Sven, *'Exterminate All the Brutes'* (Granta, 1997)

— https://www.artangel.org.uk/a-room-for-london/a-london-address/#sven-lindqvist

London, Jack, *The People of the Abyss* (1903; Tangerine Press / L-13 Light Industrial Workshop, 2014)

Nairn, Ian, *Nairn's Paris* (1968; Notting Hill Editions, 2017)

Orwell, George, 'England Your England' (1941; Penguin, 2017)

Owen, Harold, *Journey from Obscurity* (OUP, 1968)

Palmer, Christopher, *Castaway Tales: From Robinson Crusoe to Life of Pi* (Wesleyan University Press, 2016)

References

Petit, Chris, *Robinson* (Granta, 1993)

Raleigh, Walter, 'The Age of Elizabeth', in *Shakespeare's England* (Clarendon Press, 1916)

Robb, Graham, *Rimbaud* (Picador, 2000)

Robinson, Tommy, *Enemy of the State* (The Press News Ltd, 2017)

Rooper, T. G., '*Robinson Crusoe* in Education', *The Parents' Review*, June 1903

Roth, Joseph, *What I Saw: Reports from Berlin 1920–33* (trans. Michael Hofmann, Granta, 2003)

Rousseau, Jean-Jacques, *Emile, or On Education* (1762; trans. and ed. C. Kelly and A. Bloom, University Press of New England, 2010)

Selvon, Sam, *Moses Ascending* (1975; Penguin, 2008)

Shanks, Edward, *The People of the Ruins* (1920; HiLo Books, 2012)

Smith, Allan Ramsay, *Loretto School Sermons* (OUP, 1929)

Smith, Iain Crichton, *The Notebooks of Robinson Crusoe* (Gollancz, 1975)

Spark, Muriel, *Robinson* (1958; Penguin, 1964)

Spufford, Francis, ed., *The Chatto Book of Cabbages and Kings: Lists in Literature* (Chatto, 1989)

— *The Child That Books Built* (Faber, 2002)

Stasiuk, Andrzej, *Fado* (trans. Bill Johnston, Dalkey Archive, 2009)

Stevenson, Robert Louis, 'Child's Play', in *Virginibus Puerisque* (1881; Penguin, 1946)

— 'The Philosophy of Umbrellas' and 'A Gossip on Romance', in *The Lantern-Bearers and Other Essays* (selected by Jeremy Treglown, Chatto & Windus, 1988)

Taylor, D. J., *The Prose Factory: Literary Life in England since 1918* (Chatto & Windus, 2016)

Tournier, Michel, *Friday, or The Other Island* (1967; trans. Norman Denny, Penguin, 1974)

Woolf, Virginia, 'Defoe', in *The Common Reader*, Vol. 1 (1925; Vintage, 2003)

— 'Robinson Crusoe', in *The Common Reader*, Vol. 2 (1932; Vintage, 2003)

— *A Room of One's Own* (1928; Penguin, 2004)

Index of Names

CB editions

Founded in 2007, CB editions publishes chiefly
short fiction (including work by Will Eaves, Todd
McEwen and Dai Vaughan) and poetry (including
Alba Arikha, Andrew Elliott and Dan O'Brien).
Writers published in translation include Apollinaire,
Andrzej Bursa, Gert Hofmann, Agota Kristof and
Francis Ponge.

Books can be ordered from www.cbeditions.com.